ALSO BY HARVEY WASSERMAN

Harvey Wasserman's History of the United States

Harvesting Wind Energy as a Cash Crop:
A Guide to Locally Owned Wind Farming (with Dan Juhl)

The Last Energy War: The Battle Over Utility Deregulation

George W. Bush and the Death Spiral of U.S. History:
America Born & Reborn, 1620-2020 (available June 2004)

Killing Our Own: The Disaster of America's Experience With Atomic Radiation
(with Norman Solomon, Robert Alvarez and Elinor Walters)

Energy War: Reports From the Front

America Born & Reborn: The Cycles of U.S. History

ALSO BY BOB FITRAKIS

The Idea of Democratic Socialism in America
and the Decline of the Socialist Party

The Fitrakis Files: Spooks, Nukes & Nazis

The Fitrakis Files: Free Byrd & Other Cries for Justice

The Fitrakis Files: A Schoolhouse Divided

Harvey Wasserman & Bob Fitrakis

GEORGE W. BUSH vs. THE SUPERPOWER OF PEACE

How a failed Texas oilman hijacked American democracy and terrorized the world

A Columbus Institute for Contemporary Journalism Book

Published by Columbus Alive Publishing

Edited by Brian Lindamood.

The articles that appear in this collection were originally published by *Columbus Alive* and the *Columbus Free Press*, copyright © 2000-2003, reprinted with permission.

"A Prayer for America" by Dennis Kucinich, from a speech delivered to the Southern California Americans for Democratic Action, reprinted with permission.

The Columbus Institute for Contemporary Journalism is a 501(c)3 nonprofit organization.

ISBN 0-9710438-4-1

*We dedicate this book to those brave people everywhere
who devote their lives to peace, justice and ecological harmony.
They are the true SuperPower of Peace, and
with them rides our hope for survival.*

ACKNOWLEDGMENTS

This, our first collaboration together, is an anthology of columns and articles spanning 2000 to 2003, contemporaneous reports from the front lines of the battle against the Bush Junta. We are indebted to the SuperPower of Peace that both inspired and supported these writings, our website, www.freepress.org, and our journal of opinion and news analysis, the *Columbus Free Press*.

We wish to thank Congressman Dennis Kucinich for allowing us to reproduce his inspiring essay, "A Prayer for America." Its presence here does not imply that Congressman Kucinich endorses or agrees with everything we have written in the articles that appear in this anthology. It does mean that we endorse everything in the essay, and are grateful for the Congressman's untiring work for peace, justice and the American way.

We owe a major debt to our editor, Brian Lindamood at Columbus Alive Publishing, for completing this project under a severe deadline and cordially enduring our idiosyncrasies.

Our special thanks go to our webmaster extraordinaire, David Schalliol, who globalized our writings via the Internet, edited our errors and gave us frequent pep talks when the SuperPower of Peace seemed to be on the ropes.

Finally, our wonderful wives, Suzanne Patzer and Susan Wasserman, have been invaluable allies in this project. Their commitments to social justice are reflected in our writings. For true inspiration, we have also relied on our daughters, Rachel, Annie, Abbie, Julie and Shoshanna, and our pet pigs, Iggy and Winston.

CONTENTS

A PRAYER FOR AMERICA

My country 'tis of thee. Sweet land of liberty of thee I sing... From every mountain side, let freedom ring... Long may our land be bright. With freedom's holy light.

*Oh say does that Star Spangled Banner yet wave.
O'er the land of the free and the home of the brave?*

*America, America, God shed grace on thee. And crown thy good
with brotherhood from sea to shining sea.*

I offer these brief remarks today as a prayer for our country, with love of democracy, as a celebration of our country. With love for our country. With hope for our country. With a belief that the light of freedom cannot be extinguished as long as it is inside of us. With a belief that freedom rings resoundingly in a democracy each time we speak freely. With the understanding that freedom stirs the human heart and fear stills it. With the belief that a free people cannot walk in fear and faith at the same time.

With the understanding that there is a deeper truth expressed in the unity of the United States. That implicated in the union of our country is the union of all people. That all people are essentially one. That the world is interconnected not only on the material level of economics, trade, communication and transportation, but interconnected through human consciousness, through the human heart, through the heart of the world, through the simply expressed impulse and yearning to be and to breathe free. I offer this prayer for America.

Let us pray that our nation will remember that the unfolding of the promise of democracy in our nation paralleled the striving for civil rights. That is why we must challenge the rationale of the Patriot Act. We must ask, Why should America put aside guarantees of constitutional justice?

How can we justify in effect canceling the First Amendment and the right of free speech, the right to peaceably assemble? How can we justify in effect canceling the Fourth Amendment, probable cause, the prohibitions against unreasonable search and seizure? How can we justify in effect canceling the Fifth Amendment, nullifying due process, and allowing for indefinite incarceration without a trial? How can we justify in effect canceling the Sixth Amendment, the right to prompt and public trial? How can we justify in effect canceling the Eighth Amendment, which protects against cruel and unusual punishment?

We cannot justify widespread wiretaps and Internet surveillance without judicial supervision, let alone with it. We cannot justify secret searches without a warrant. We cannot justify giving the Attorney General the ability to designate domestic terror groups. We cannot justify giving the FBI total access to any type of data which may exist in any system anywhere, such as medical records and financial records.

We cannot justify giving the CIA the ability to target people in this country for intelligence surveillance. We cannot justify a government which takes from the people our right to privacy and then assumes for its own operations a right to total secrecy. The Attorney General recently covered up a statue of Lady Justice showing her bosom as if to underscore there is no danger of justice exposing herself at this time, before this administration.

Let us pray that our nation's leaders will not be overcome with fear. Because today there is great fear in our great Capitol. And this must be understood before we can ask about the shortcomings of Congress in the current environment.

The great fear began when we had to evacuate the Capitol on September 11. It continued when we had to leave the Capitol again when a bomb scare occurred as members were pressing the CIA during a secret briefing. It continued when we abandoned Washington when anthrax, possibly from a government lab, arrived in the mail. It continued when the Attorney General declared a nationwide terror alert and then the administration brought the destructive Patriot Bill to the floor of the House. It continued in the release of the bin Laden tapes at the same time the President was announcing the withdrawal from the ABM treaty.

It remains present in the cordoning off of the Capitol. It is present in the camouflaged armed National Guardsmen who greet members of Congress each day we enter the Capitol campus. It is present in the labyrinth of concrete barriers through which we must pass each time we go to vote. The trappings of a state of siege trap us in a state of fear, ill equipped to deal with the Patriot Games, the Mind Games, the War Games of an unelected President and his unelected Vice President.

Let us pray that our country will stop this war. "To promote the common defense" is one of the formational principles of America. Our Congress gave the President the ability to respond to the tragedy of September 11. We licensed a response to those who helped bring the terror of September 11. But we the people and our elected representatives must reserve the right to measure the response, to proportion the response, to challenge the response, and to correct the response.

Because we did not authorize the invasion of Iraq.

We did not authorize the invasion of Iran.

We did not authorize the invasion of North Korea.

We did not authorize the bombing of civilians in Afghanistan.

We did not authorize permanent detainees in Guantanamo Bay.

We did not authorize the withdrawal from the Geneva Convention.

We did not authorize military tribunals suspending due process and habeas corpus.

We did not authorize assassination squads.

We did not authorize the resurrection of COINTELPRO.

We did not authorize the repeal of the Bill of Rights.

We did not authorize the revocation of the Constitution.

We did not authorize national identity cards.

We did not authorize the eye of Big Brother to peer from cameras throughout our cities.

We did not authorize an eye for an eye. Nor did we ask that the blood of innocent people, who perished on September 11, be avenged with the blood of innocent villagers in Afghanistan.

We did not authorize the administration to wage war anytime, anywhere, anyhow it pleases.

We did not authorize war without end.

We did not authorize a permanent war economy.

Yet we are upon the threshold of a permanent war economy. The President has requested a $45.6 billion increase in military spending. All defense-related programs will cost close to $400 billion. Consider that the Department of Defense has never passed an independent audit. Consider that the Inspector General has notified Congress that the Pentagon cannot properly account for $1.2 trillion in transactions. Consider that in recent years the Department of Defense could not match $22 billion worth of expenditures to the items it purchased, wrote off as lost billions of dollars worth of in-transit inventory, and stored nearly $30 billion worth of spare parts it did not need.

Yet the defense budget grows with more money for weapons systems to fight a cold war which ended, weapon systems in search of new enemies to create new wars. This has nothing to do with fighting terror. This has everything to do with fueling a military-industrial machine with the treasure of our nation, risking the future of our nation, risking democracy itself with the militarization of thought which follows the militarization of the budget.

Let us pray for our children. Our children deserve a world without end. Not a war without end. Our children deserve a world free of the terror of hunger, free of the terror of poor health care, free of the terror of homelessness, free of the terror of ignorance, free of the terror of hopelessness, free of the terror of policies which are committed to a world view which is not appropriate for the survival of a free people, not appropriate for the survival of democratic values, not appropriate for the survival of our nation, and not appropriate for the survival of the world.

Let us pray that we have the courage and the will as a people and as a nation to shore ourselves up, to reclaim our democratic traditions from the ruins of September 11. Let us declare our love for democracy. Let us declare our intent for peace. Let us work to make nonviolence an organizing principle in our own society. Let us recommit ourselves to the slow and painstaking work of statecraft, which sees peace, not war, as being inevitable. Let us work for a world where someday war becomes archaic.

That is the vision which the proposal to create a Department of Peace envisions. Forty-three members of Congress are now cosponsoring the legislation. Let us work for a world where nuclear disarmament is an imperative. That is why we must begin by insisting on the commitments of the ABM treaty. That is why we must be steadfast for nonproliferation.

Let us work for a world where America can lead the way in banning weapons of mass destruction not only from our land and sea and sky but from outer-space itself. That is the vision of HR 3616: A universe free of fear. Where we can look up at God's creation in the stars and imagine infinite wisdom, infinite peace, infinite possibilities, not infinite war, because we are taught that the kingdom will come on earth as it is in heaven.

Let us pray that we have the courage to replace the images of death which haunt us, the layers of images of September 11, faded into images of patriotism, spliced into images of military mobilization, jump-cut into images of our secular celebrations of the World Series, New Year's Eve, the Superbowl, the Olympics, the strobic flashes which touch our deepest fears. Let us replace those images with the work of human relations, reaching out to people, helping our own citizens here at home, lifting the plight of the poor everywhere. That is the America which has the ability to rally the support of the world. That is the America which stands not in pursuit of an axis of evil, but which is itself at the axis of hope and faith and peace and freedom.

America, America. God shed grace on thee. Crown thy good, America. Not with weapons of mass destruction. Not with invocations of an axis of evil. Not through breaking international treaties. Not through establishing America as king of a unipolar world. Crown thy good America.

America, America. Let us pray for our country. Let us love our country. Let us defend our country not only from the threats without but from the threats within. Crown thy good, America. Crown thy good with brotherhood, and sisterhood. And crown thy good with compassion and restraint and forbearance and a commitment to peace, to democracy, to economic justice here at home and throughout the world. Crown thy good, America. Crown thy good America. Crown thy good.

TRUTH IS THE WEAPON OF BUSH'S SELF-DESTRUCTION

The Bush assault is foundering on the shoals of Truth. The Republicans have seized control of the American judicial, legislative and executive branches. Their immensely effective corporate mass media misinform, mislead and manipulate. They control the world's most powerful army, and are glad to use it without provocation.

Having stolen the election of 2000, Bush's minions are rigging America's voting machines and erasing countless suspected Democrats from voter rolls. Their goal is to shock and awe the opposition into extinction. If "image is everything," Bush sits atop a dictatorial fortress, not likely to fall soon.

But history teaches that, ultimately, Truth is more powerful than image: All the people can't be fooled all the time.

Globally, George W. Bush has become history's most hated U.S. President. After being gifted near-total support by Osama bin Laden, Bush has sunk to unprecedented scorn. In the global village, American's unelected chief is under quarantine.

Why? Because outside the U.S., the Truth is being told. The world media and the Internet seethe with serious reporting and outrage against escalating deceit. In the U.S., the corporate media have polluted the

1

information flow. So we are compelled, more than ever, to compile and refute the lies, and to spread their antidote far and wide. Our arsenal of Truth includes:

Saddam's WMD: Obviously, if he had weapons of mass destruction, he would have used them. It took years for the lies about the Vietnamese non-attack at Tonkin Gulf to unravel; it's taken mere days to establish that Bush blatantly lied in no less a venue than the State of the Union. Who will believe him next time?

Saddam's nukes: He had none, and Colin Powell lied to the United Nations and the world based on forgeries. Who will believe him next time?

Bogus intelligence: The Republicans forced intelligence operatives to sacrifice their credibility to provide a pretext for war. Who will believe them next time?

Saddam hated Osama: The devout fundamentalist Osama bin Laden hated the secular Saddam Hussein, who returned the sentiment. That these sworn enemies could have worked together on September 11 was yet another calculated lie.

The real reasons for war: Bush used terrorism, WMDs and (incredibly) human rights as pretexts for war in Iraq and Afghanistan. But everything since has confirmed what the world knew all along: it's about oil and the pipelines to carry it, with some Christian fanaticism thrown in.

Spinning Private Lynch: This contrived mocku-drama, complete with threats from the Pentagon against reporters (such as Robert Scheer of the *Los Angeles Times*) who document what really happened, was in fact a tale of Iraqi bravery and compassion.

"Top Gun": Bush's handlers blew a million taxpayer dollars to spin an aircraft carrier so Bush could play Tom Cruise. That jump suit now symbolizes chickenhawk hypocrisy.

An AWOL war record: Bush deserted his cushy National Guard unit, then joked that raising twins was harder than being in combat, which he never saw.

Mission accomplished: Neither Afghanistan nor Iraq has been liberated or conquered. The "dancing in the streets" promised by the wars' perpetrators has become a desert Vietnam, where locals and Americans continue to die.

September 11: The terrorist attacks occurred while George W. Bush was officially responsible for protecting the American people. His bitter fight against a full congressional investigation betrays something very serious to hide.

Flaunting tragedy: To the horror of many September 11 victims' families, Bush has manipulated the terrorist attacks into what he called a personal political "trifecta," desecrating the sacrifice of 3,000 innocent civilians.

Attacking the heroes: While praising police and firefighter heroes, Bush slashed their benefits and attacked their (and others') unions. Meanwhile, on the brink of the Iraq attack and amid "support our troops" rallying cries, the Republicans slashed veterans' benefits by nearly $30 billion.

Homeland security: To fund tax cuts for the rich, the security of America's ports, airports and borders has been compromised, and they may be less safe than before September 11.

Internal security: Using September 11 as pretext, Bush has shredded the Bill of Rights, with no gain for public safety. But the USA Patriot Act and other limits on American freedom have become powerful weapons to use against his opponents.

Official secrecy: Bush is the most secretive U.S. president ever. His relentless campaign against open government belies much to hide.

Home of the free: While claiming to spread "American freedom," Bush keeps two million citizens in jail, a quarter of all the world's prisoners, 40 percent of them held on victimless drug charges.

Guantanamo: While claiming to spread "American freedom," Bush has established a concentration camp on conquered land where human rights are shredded in contempt for global treaties, and where a death chamber may soon be added.

The tax cut: Selling a handout to the rich as a stimulus package, and lying about its true cost, Bush surreptitiously doomed the Social Security, Medicare and Medicaid programs that have been the backbone of American social democracy.

Jobs, jobs, jobs: Bush's mantra about job creation has proved a hollow lie as the economy continues to slide, with Hoover-esque joblessness and homelessness soaring in traditional Republican style.

Limited government: While campaigning against "big government" Bush has pushed official spying into every corner of American private life, including reproductive rights and our ability to choose what to smoke and whom to marry. In fact, Bush supports limiting the government's power only when it comes to regulating his corporate cronies.

An American theocracy: Empowered by the hellish marriage of corporate power with right-wing Christian fundamentalism, separation of church and state has disappeared in a global "crusade" that uses taxpayer money to support reactionary churches and the concept of an American ayatollah.

Armageddon countdown: Bush's foreign policy , especially in the Middle East, features a psychotic sectarian belief in an "end of days" scenario where a chosen few with a peculiar view of Christ ascend to a very private Heaven, leaving the rest of us to burn.

States' rights: While arguing for states' rights, Bush sends federal troops to arrest harmless pot smokers in states that have legalized medical marijuana.

The role of government: While endorsing a wide range of government functions (like providing security), Bush really supports just three: funding the military, subsidizing client corporations, and suppressing opposition.

A free-market economy: While mouthing the platitudes of Adam Smith, Bush demands huge bailouts for nuclear power and the other obsolete, polluting industries that fund his campaigns.

Education: While claiming to support education, Bush is robbing Head Start to fund further tax cuts for his fellow rich.

Personal finances: Bush's road to wealth is littered with Enron-style insider trading, especially at Harken Energy and the Texas Rangers, which have avoided media scrutiny while making Martha Stewart seem a piker.

A popular President: Bush lost the 2000 election by 500,000 votes and his approval ratings regularly sag between crises, but the corporate media grovel over his alleged "popularity" while refusing to pursue anything that would seriously damage him.

An affable President: Bush's good ol' boy veneer hides the meanness of spirit and coarse ruthlessness essential to a corporate-fundamentalist attack on civil society.

A Teflon President: Like Ronald Reagan (and unlike Bill Clinton) the media refusal to pursue damaging (and felonious) presidential misdeeds guarantees Bush a free ride. Or does it?

Bush's litany of lies grows daily. In the short term, they demoralize the opposition.

The mainstream media does its part by dismissing those abundant, articulate critics who don't, like Paul Wellstone, conveniently wind up dead. But in a world that demands non-violent resistance, there is no alternative to perseverance, and no greater weapon than an adversary's own lies.

It took a world war and 40 million deaths to rid the world of the Nazi plague. Thus far Bush has killed thousands to conquer Afghanistan and Iraq, and shows no compunction about killing more. His environmental and other policies have doomed millions worldwide, and threaten the life support systems on which we all depend.

But the SuperPower of Truth can number his days.

It's been said a lie can circle the globe before Truth gets its boots on. But once shod, Truth and only Truth can crush tyrants, kick down prison doors and walk the world back into the sunshine of freedom.

Bush himself has handed an organized, focused and optimistic SuperPower of Peace the tools it needs to get stomping.

So let's roll.

PART ONE

STOLEN ELECTION, STOLEN NATION

DARK SIDE
OF THE
MOON

After Texas Governor George W. Bush faltered in New Hampshire in early 2000, a shadowy right-wing network came to his rescue in South Carolina, turning a certain primary defeat into a double-digit victory. As the *Washington Post* noted, "An array of conservative groups have come in to reinforce Bush's message with phone banks, radio ads and mailings of their own."

Washington Post columnist Richard Cohen asserted that "Bush embraces the far-right fringe." From the racists who prohibit interracial dating at Bob Jones University to the moronic Confederate flag wavers, from Rush Limbaugh to Pat Robertson, and from the most extreme elements of the right-to-life movement to the Moonies, the Bush family network prevailed. NBC's Tim Russert pointed out that George W. was now "indebted to Pat Robertson, Jerry Falwell" and the Christian right.

Dutifully, the *Washington Times*—a paper owned by self-proclaimed messiah and cult leader Reverend Sun Myung Moon—ran a headline stating, "Bush scoffs at the assertion he moved too far right." The bizarre and almost unbelievable relationship between the Bush family and the 80-year-old Moon is the dirty little secret of Bush's campaign for President.

To understand the role the Moonies play in U.S. politics, one must start with Ryoichi Sasakawa, identified in a 1992 PBS *Frontline* investigative report as a key money source for Reverend Moon's far-flung world empire. In the 1930s, Sasakawa was one of Japan's leading fascists. He organized a private army of 1,500 men equipped with 20 warplanes. His men dressed in black shirts to emulate Mussolini. Sasakawa was an "uncondemned Class-A war criminal" suddenly freed with another accused war criminal— Yoshio Kodama, a leading figure in Japan's organized crime syndicate Yakuza—in 1948.

In January 1995, Japan's KYODO news service uncovered documents establishing that the one-time fascist war criminal suspect was earmarked as an informer by U.S. military intelligence two months prior to his unexplained release. Declassified documents link Kodama's release to the CIA. During World War II, the Kodama Agency, according to U.S. Army counterintelligence records, consisted of "systematically looting China of its raw materials" and dealing in heroin, guns, tungsten, gold, industrial diamonds and radium.

Both Sasakawa and Kodama's CIA ties are a reoccurring theme in their relationship with the Moonies. In 1977, Congressman Donald Fraser launched an investigation into Moon's background. The 444-page Congressional report alleged Moonie involvement with bribery, bank fraud, illegal kickbacks and arms sales. The report revealed that Moon's 20,000-member Unification Church was a creation of Korean Central Intelligence Agency (KCIA) Director Kim Chong Phil as a political tool to influence U.S. foreign policy. The U.S. CIA was the agency primarily responsible for the founding of the KCIA.

The Moon organizations have denied any links with the Korean government or intelligence community.

Moon, who is Korean, and his two Japanese buddies, Sasakawa and Kodama, first joined together in the 1960s to form the Asian People's Anti-Communist League with the aid of KCIA agents, alleged Japanese organized crime money and financial support from Chinese Generalissimo Chiang Kai-Shek. The League concentrated on uniting fascists, right-wing and anti-Communist forces throughout Asia.

In 1964, League funds set up Moon's Freedom Center in the United States. Kodama served as chief advisor to the Moon subsidiary Win Over Communism, an organization that served to protect Moon's South Korean investments. Sasakawa acted as Win Over Communism's chair.

In 1966, the League merged with the anti-Bolshevik Bloc of Nations, another group with strong fascist ties, to form the World Anti-Communist League (WACL). Later, in the 1980s, the retired U.S. Major General John Singlaub emerged as a key player in the Iran-Contra scandal through his chairmanship of the WACL. Singlaub enlisted paramilitary groups, foreign governments and right-wing Americans to support the Contra cause in Nicaragua.

Moon's Freedom Center served as the headquarters for the League in the United States. During the Iran-Contra hearings, the League was described as "a multi-national network of Nazi war criminals, Latin American death squad leaders, North American racists and anti-Semites and fascist politicians from every continent."

Working with the KCIA, Moon made his first trip to the U.S. in 1965 and obtained an audience with former President Dwight D. Eisenhower. Ike, along with former President Harry S Truman, lent their names to the letterhead of the Moon-created Korean Cultural Freedom Foundation. In 1969, Moon and Sasakawa jointly formed the Freedom Leadership Foundation, a pro-Vietnam War organization that lobbied the U.S. government.

In the 1970s, Moon earned notoriety in the Koreagate scandal after female followers of the Unification Church were accused of entertaining and keeping confidential files on several U.S. congressmen who they "lobbied" at a Washington Hilton Hotel suite rented by the Moonies. The U.S. Senate held hearings concerning Moon's "programmatic bribery of U.S. officials, journalists and others as part of an operation by the Korean CIA to influence the course of U.S. foreign policy."

The Fraser report noted that Moon was paid by the KCIA to stage demonstrations at the United Nations and run pro-South Korean propaganda campaigns. The Congressional investigator for the Fraser report said, "We determined that their [Moonies'] primary interest, at least in the U.S. at that time, was not religious at all but was political, it was attempt to gain power, influence and authority."

After Ronald Reagan's presidential victory in 1980, Moon's political influence increased dramatically. Vice President George Bush, a former CIA director, invited Moon as his guest to the Reagan inauguration. Bush and Moon shared unsavory links to South American underworld figures. In 1980, according to the investigatory magazine *IF*, the Moon organization collaborated with a right-wing military coup in Bolivia that established the region's first narco-state.

Moon's credentials soared in conservative circles in 1982 with the inception of the *Washington Times*. Vice President Bush immediately saw the value of building an alliance with the politically powerful Moon organization, an alliance that Moon claims made Bush President. One ex-Moonie's website claims that during the 1988 Bush-Dukakis battle, Reverend Moon threatened his followers that he'd move all of them out of the U.S. if the evil Dukakis won.

Also in 1982, Moon was convicted of income tax evasion and spent more than a year in jail.

During the first Gulf War, the Moonie-sponsored American Freedom Coalition organized "support the troop" rallies. The *Frontline* documentary identified the *Washington Times* as the most costly piece in Moon's propaganda arsenal, with losses estimated as high as $800 million. Still, Sasakawa's virtual monopoly over the Japanese speedboat gambling industry allowed the money to continue flowing to Moon's U.S. coffers.

The Bush-Moonie connection caused considerable controversy in September 1995, when the former President announced he would be spending nearly a week in Japan on behalf of a Moonie front organization, the Women's Federation for World Peace, founded and led by Moon's wife. Bush downplayed accusations of brain-washing and coercion against the Moonies. The *New York Times* noted that Bush's presence "is seen by some as lending the group [Moonies] legitimacy."

Longtime Moonie member S.P. Simonds wrote an editorial for the *Portland Press Herald* noting the Bushes "didn't need the reported million dollars paid by Moon and were well aware of the Church's history."

Bush shared the podium with Moon's wife and addressed a crowd of 50,000 in the Tokyo dome. Bush told the true believers, "Reverend and Mrs. Moon are engaged in the most important activities going on in the world today."

The following year Moon bankrolled a series of "family values" conferences from Oakland to Washington, D.C. The *San Francisco Chronicle* reported, "In Washington, Moon opened his checkbook to such Republican Party mainstays as former Presidents Gerald Ford and George Bush, GOP presidential candidate Jack Kemp and Christian Coalition leader Ralph Reed."

Purdue University Professor of Sociology Anson Shupe, a longtime Moon watcher, said, "The man accused of being the biggest brainwasher in America has moved into mainstream Republican Americana."

Moon claimed at these family values conferences that he was the "only one who knows all the secrets of God." One of them, according to the *Chronicle*, is that "the husband is the owner of his wife's sexual organs and vice versa."

"President Ford, President Bush, who attended the Inaugural World Convention of the Family Federation for World Peace and all you distinguished guests are famous, but there's something that you do not know," the *Chronicle* quoted Moon as saying. "Is there anyone here who dislikes sexual organs?... Until now you may not have thought it virtuous to value the sexual organs, but from now, you must value them."

In November 1996, Bush arrived in Buenos Aires, Argentina, amid controversy over a newly created Spanish-language Moon weekly newspaper called *Tiempos del Mundo*. Bush smoothed things over as the principal speaker at the paper's opening dinner on November 23.

The former President then traveled with Moon to neighboring Uruguay to help him open a Montevideo seminary to train 4,200 young Japanese women to spread the word of the Unification Church across Latin America. The young Japanese seminarians were later accused of laundering $80 million through an Uruguayan bank, according to the *St. Petersburg Times*.

The *Times* also reported that when Reverend Jerry Falwell's university faced bankruptcy, Moon's group bailed it out with millions of dollars in loans and grants.

The *New York Times* noted in 1997 that Moon "has been reaching out to conservative Christians in this country in the last few years by emphasizing shared goals like support for sexual abstinence outside of marriage and opposition to homosexuality." Moon also appeals to the Second Amendment crowd. In March 1999, the *Washington Post* reported that the messiah owned the lucrative Kahr Arms Company through Saeilo Inc.

It's the shadowy network around the Moonies that the elder Bush could have called in to bail out his son's campaign in South Carolina. Make no mistake, George W. of Texas is little more than a frontman for the restoration of his father's unsavory connections, who hide behind the veil of national security to avoid accountability.

FITRAKIS
November 16, 2000

UNANSWERED EXIT POLL QUESTIONS

T he mainstream media's self-flagellation for calling the Florida election early—first for Gore, then for Bush—may be misplaced. Projections based on exit polls using advanced sampling methods have almost never failed before. Maybe the media's initial exit polls were correct this time too.

Suppose in the recent Yugoslavian election we learned that the exit polls predicted Slobodan Milosevich's opponent as the victor; there were massive voting irregularities in the one area of the country controlled by Milosevich's brother; it turns out that Milosevich's father was the former director of the secret police, who previously manipulated elections throughout the world; and Milosevich is suddenly winning by a few hundred votes.

What would we think? We'd immediately suspect a coup d'etat and a stolen election. We'd call for a United Nations-supervised recount and dispatch the U.S. Secretary of State to oversee it.

Here in the U.S. election, we have a presidential candidate with the most votes—a clear plurality of 500,000 votes over his opponent—who's losing because of a few hundred votes in one state. The mainstream media drumbeat is trying to force popular vote winner Al Gore to concede the race "for the good of the country" while spinning stories on how the early projections of a Gore victory were wrong. But it's entirely plausible that the exit polls in Florida were correct—people came out of the voting booths saying that they voted for Gore, not knowing that their votes would be counted otherwise.

Gore was leading in the exit polls in Florida, a state controlled by his opponent's brother, Governor Jeb Bush. It turns out their father is the former U.S. CIA director who manipulated scores of elections throughout the Third World in the mid 1970s. George W. Bush appears to be ahead by a few hundred votes in Florida. And two former U.S. Secretary of States were dispatched to oversee the recount.

But it's the United States, not Yugoslavia. There couldn't be a coup d'e-tat here. Could there?

Maybe there's a reason why it's so important to the Bush family that one of their own holds the power of the presidency next year. Long-awaited CIA files tying former CIA Director George Bush to human rights abuses and other potential crimes are to be released to the public next year—particularly the elder Bush's alleged role in the double homicide of Chilean dissident Orlando Letelier and U.S. ally Ronnie Moffitt in a 1976 Washington, D.C., car bombing. The next President of the United States will be the one to decide if these files are released in a timely manner.

Senator Frank Church's 1975 congressional investigation of the CIA's covert activities found that the organization had run between 10,000 and 20,000 covert operations in its four decades. The most common of these operations was rigging elections, not surprisingly often by directing votes to obscure third-party candidates.

The question the American media doesn't want to ask is the most obvious: Did the Bushes bring their unique covert election-rigging skills to the Banana Republic of Florida?

It's an issue that the world press is not afraid to tackle, as seen in some excerpts collected by *Newsweek* this week. "U.S. Humiliated in Presidential Shambles," screamed the page-one headline on Britain's *The Mirror*. "The health certificate of the greatest democracy in the world includes, unquestionably, some serious black marks," wrote France's *Le Monde*. Italy's *La Repubblica* commented that the atmosphere in the U.S. is "not so much of a superpower but of a super banana republic."

Doesn't it make you proud to be an American?

ONLY GORE IS TO BLAME

The Bush Republicans have stolen another election. And the Gore Democrats will blame Ralph Nader for it, when they have only themselves to fault. In fact, Nader showed the Dems how to win the presidency, and they didn't do it.

Al Gore was a miserable candidate who ran a miserable campaign. But he still managed to win a 500,000-vote plurality nationwide, even above the 2.6 million votes won by Nader.

Gore also carried Florida. Until the TV networks were reversed by a Bush first cousin strategically perched at Fox News, the networks correctly surmised early on election night that Gore had won the Sunshine State. The projections were based on sophisticated exit polls that counted the intent of the vast majority of south Florida blacks and Jews who voted Democratic, especially in Palm Beach County.

How could the networks know the ballots in Governor Jeb Bush's state would be sabotaged and left uncounted? Or that blacks trying to vote throughout Florida were being racially profiled by Republican election officials demanding additional identification and even preventing them—Jim Crow style—from getting to the polls at all? The Republicans systematically disenfranchised more than enough blacks and Jews to give the

White House to George W. Bush.

The Shrub may or may not win all the court challenges. But ultimately the right-wing Florida legislature and the Republican-controlled Congress will guarantee he succeeds his father after this eight-year Clinton interruptus.

Gore is right to keep up the battle. The one thing his bulldog nature has proven good for is guaranteeing that every stone will be lifted in tracking down those disenfranchised votes. His quest will ultimately be futile, though hopefully some electoral reform will come out of it.

But the one reform that must come—limiting the ability of corporations to buy elections—undoubtedly will not. Big Money spent some $2 billion placing its markers on the future White House, Congress, state and local governments this year. Bush endorsed that purchase. Gore endorsed the McCain-Feingold reform package, a limited start.

The only credible attack came from Nader, who's spent his life fighting the corporations that bought this election. This is ultimately why he was marginalized, especially by the major media, the primary profit center created by all that corrupt largess.

While Bush spent more than $300 million, and Gore more than $200 million, Nader spent about $3 million. Yet the entire election turned on the 66-year-old activist who flew coach with his nephew and charged admission to his speeches. Enough people voted for Nader in Florida (and New Hampshire) who might otherwise have voted for Gore to turn the election (assuming their votes would have been counted).

So how did it happen?

Nader had two primary goals: to be included in the debates, and to get five percent of the vote to qualify the Green Party for matching campaign funds. He also had a few points to make along the way about the environment, consumer issues and money in politics.

Nader pioneered the consumer movement, has been a mainstay of the environmental movement, and has trained an entire generation of activists—including many at the core of today's Democratic Party. He was the Green Party nominee in 1996. Though he barely campaigned, he got more than a million votes. It was well known for four years that he would run again in 2000, and probably do a better job of it.

In 1993, Nader met with the new Vice President and offered to convene a national gathering of environmental activists to meet with Gore. Nader wrote Gore a dozen times, called him still more. Though the veep found time to meet with hundreds of corporate funders, he never again met with Nader.

In 1996, the Democrats completely ignored the Green Party, even though Nader's non-campaign drew a million-plus votes and Green organizing proved key in several close Congressional and local elections.

In 2000, the Democrats also tried to ignore the Greens. But they had a problem with the labor movement. By ramming the anti-union, anti-green North American Free Trade Agreement through Congress, Clinton and Gore embittered labor activists. Key union presidents took pains to be photographed with Nader, who was NAFTA's most eloquent opponent. Though the union leadership soon went back to Gore, much of the rank and file didn't. They either didn't vote for him or didn't campaign for him, refusing to provide the grassroots boost Democrats always count on at election time. By most counts, more than 35 percent of the union members who voted went for Bush. About four percent went for Nader.

At the Democratic National Convention, Gore seemed to finally realize he had a problem on the left. His superb acceptance speech hammered at issues carefully designed to reclaim labor, defuse green opposition and energize the grassroots campaign needed to beat the Bush money machine. He emerged from the convention 15 points ahead. His election seemed secure. As David Letterman put it: "Only Al Gore can beat Al Gore."

And he did. He drifted back to the right. Gore's floundering autumn non-campaign consisted primarily of losing three debates to the dumbest and least-qualified major party candidate since Warren G. Harding. While putting America to sleep with the minutiae of his tax plans, Gore inspired exactly no one.

At the same time, Gore said nothing about Nader being excluded from the debates. Nader was even physically ejected from the audience of the first one. We'll never know how those debates might have gone had Nader been included, but they couldn't have been worse for Gore.

Meanwhile, Nader rallied the green base with compelling hour-long lectures which thousands of college students and gray-haired activists paid money to hear. Deftly combining celebrity music with actual content, Nader persuaded armies of young people to vote for the first time, and hordes more to work for a new Green Party instead of the old Democrats.

It was only after Gore blew his debates with Bush that the Democrats suddenly seemed to care that Nader was running. Refusing for seven years to meet with America's leading consumer advocate was not enough. The Dems—with a scant few weeks remaining in the election—suddenly demanded Nader's three decades of consistent organizing be trashed for Gore's benefit.

It was an impossible demand, but it was heeded. Left media like *The Nation* and *Progressive* magazines filled with angst. The left loves nothing more than a circular firing squad, and the accusations began flying. Thousands ultimately opted to "trade" their Nader votes in projected swing states like Florida and Ohio for Gore votes in safe ones like Massachusetts and New York.

But Gore did everything he could to make matters worse. Instead of actually courting the green vote, he went on the attack, with his minions accusing the long-scorned enviros of virtual treason.

Most telling was Clinton administration's staunch refusal to shut the WTI toxic waste burner in East Liverpool, Ohio. Campaigning in 1992, the Democrats promised that if elected, this lethal facility would never open. That promise was credited by many with the Clinton/Gore ticket having carried Ohio. But the plant not only opened, it continues to operate eight years later. An EPA report gave the administration a golden opportunity to shut WTI just prior to the 2000 election. But it didn't happen.

After eight years in office, the administration's environmental legacy was so thin that Bush the oil man was able to fault Gore for—of all things—not having established an energy policy. No one doubted Gore would be "better than Bush" on the environment, as well as on a host of other progressive issues. But the Gore idea of winning the environmental vote was to beat up on both Bush and Nader—reserving the harshest attacks for Nader—and to do nothing to rally grassroots green and labor and first-time voters to his side.

That Nader could consistently outdraw both Bush and Gore was not Nader's "fault," any more than he was responsible for Bill Clinton's dalliance with Monica Lewinsky. Nor was Nader responsible for Gore losing his own state of Tennessee or Clinton's Arkansas, or the once-permanent Democratic stronghold of West Virginia.

Indeed, the few hundred thousand Nader votes that might otherwise have gone to Gore pale in comparison to the sink hole of the Clinton presidency, and the colossal mishandling of the Gore campaign. Though the

Republicans managed to stir plenty of ire with their absurd impeachment assault, it was the Clinton Democrats who most thoroughly sabotaged Gore's election attempt.

While the New Democrats crowed about having won the White House by negating traditional Democrat ideology, that also cost them this election. While turning themselves into moderate Republicans, the Clinton Democrats not only necessitated the rise of the Green Party, they dispirited the Dems' natural grassroots base, which came alive after Gore's populist convention speech, only to disappear again in the fall.

The New Democrats also directly disenfranchised hundreds of thousands of black voters thanks to their unconscionable drug war. Even as you read this, the Clinton administration has taken the state of California to the U.S. Supreme Court, demanding that the voters' approval of the use of medical marijuana be negated. When doctors in the Bay Area began prescribing pot for AIDS and cancer patients, Clinton sent troopers in to make arrests and threaten the doctors' licenses.

Some two million Americans (and a disproportionate number of African-Americans) are now in jail, the world's largest prison population. At least 40 percent are there for drug-related arrests. As a result, hundreds of thousands of African-Americans have lost their right to vote due to felony convictions.

That includes some 160,000 black males in Florida. If national trends held there, more than 80 percent of them would have voted for Gore, dwarfing the Nader vote, and providing thousands more votes than would have been needed to carry the state.

Thankfully, Bush will enter the White House as the first president since 1888 without even a plurality of the national vote. He came in second out of four. And he will govern under the cloud of having clearly stolen the electoral vote.

Yet even at that, it did not have to be. Lewinsky. NAFTA. WTI. The drug war. You name it. Mainstream Democrats can scapegoat Ralph Nader all they want. But in the coming dark years, in the shadow of the Shrub, there's only Al Gore and his New Democrats to blame.

THE IDIOT BASTARD SON

Repeat the mantra: "George W. Bush is the legitimate President of the United States, the legitimate President of the United States, the legitimate President of the United States..."

Never has the mainstream media been more naked and desperate in its attempts to "manufacture consent," a term coined by brilliant linguist Noam Chomsky. Not since three separate lone gunmen just happened to shoot the Kennedy brothers and Martin Luther King Jr. have we witnessed such brazen Orwellian coersion. But as the mega-corporate pundits of America attempt to pressure every dissenting voice to repeat the legitimacy refrain, facts keep filtering out that suggest the exact opposite.

Let's take the word legitimacy. In medieval times, it meant what it implies: the king or heir apparent was not literally a bastard, as in the movie *Braveheart*, but his royal parents were his actual biological parents. Under modern democracy, the term implies that you won the election legitimately, at a minimum: the adult population could vote, those votes were fairly counted, and you got the most votes.

We know legitimate voters were prevented from voting in Florida. Republican Secretary of State and Bush loyalist Katherine Harris hired the Republican company ChoicePoint, and their subsidiary Database

Technologies, to ethnically and racially "cleanse" (their word) Florida's voter registration rolls. According to Bob Herbert of the *New York Times*, the companies now admit that they accidentally purged 8,000 voters from the rolls who weren't felons, overwhelmingly from poor and minority districts, who were eligible to vote.

Take the case of Dave Crawford of Broward County who showed up at the polls with his five-year-old daughter and was reportedly told by the kindly Southern election official, "Son, we've got a problem. You're not allowed to vote. Son, says here you're a convict. Convicts can't vote." Despite the fact Crawford had never been arrested in his life, the election official refused to show Crawford the felon list and turned him away from the poll, with his daughter crying.

We know all votes were not fairly counted. A one-vote majority of the Supreme Court stopped the counting of ballots at the state and local level for the first time in U.S. history. The absurdity of a 14th Amendment "equal protection" argument should not be lost. In a state where there are a variety of voting devices in different counties—and the minority and poor precincts get the worst machines, which fail to count four percent of the vote, while the rich precincts get optical scanners which count over 99 percent of all the vote—how can there be a single state standard?

The Florida Supreme Court has always interpreted Florida statute to mean a "reasonable" standard for each county. Bush's own expert witness, John Ahmann, conceded that the Votomatic machines used in the poorest county are prone to failure and can only be corrected through hand counting.

For the five Bushwhackers on the Supreme Court to be concerned about the impossibility of setting a statewide standard of recounting—instead of being concerned about actually counting votes—is both surreal and hypocritical. That's why Justice John Paul Stevens' comments in his dissent are so important. "Counting every legally cast vote cannot constitute irreparable harm," he said. What created irreparable harm was not counting every vote.

It's estimated that 187,000 votes went uncounted in Florida, with more than half of them in black precincts. Even the pathetic Republican counter-argument that votes also weren't counted in Republican counties are blatant distortions. What they won't tell you about the 25,000 votes thrown out by the Duval County canvassing board is that 17,000 came from the black precincts.

Also, in order to keep the votes from being counted, Bush essentially rented a riot of 150 Republican operatives who stormed the Miami Dade canvassing board to stop the recount. The *Wall Street Journal* reported that the plane tickets and hotel rooms for the demonstrators were paid for by Republican funders and that the President-select called and joked with the "Rent-A-Riot" crowd at an after-protest party where Las Vegas lounge lizard Wayne Newton serenaded them with "Danke Schoen."

We know Gore won the popular vote. The exit polls on election night were right, regardless of Bush's cousin reversing the call on Fox TV. Most projections have Gore winning Florida if all the ballots were counted—by between 23,000 to 57,000 votes. That's why Bush loyalists are busy trying to seal those uncounted ballots "for the good of the country." Remember, they also sealed the JFK, MLK and RFK files to help the country. Thanks. Reality's a tough thing to deal with in a democracy.

The President-select, George W. Bush, has a huge "legitimacy gap." The words to the mid-1960s Zappa song keep coming to mind, "The idiot bastard son, his daddy's a Nazi in Congress today." The son grew up, and despite double-legacy Ivy League-style affirmative action—and even though his daddy is the former CIA director and President—the bastard appears to be as idiotic as ever.

It should strike people as odd that after apparently stealing an election through the state apparatus controlled by Bush's governor brother, his loyalists would immediately demand that everybody kiss the ring of legitimacy. I'll be first to admit that the Bush family stole it fair and square, and they might have been owed one after the Kennedy boys' handiwork in 1960. But to pretend that the Bushes didn't steal it through the systematic disenfranchisement of blacks, Jews, Hispanics and poor people in Florida—please, my brothers and sisters.

If Bush wants legitimacy, he's going to have to earn it the old-fashioned way, through real policy initiatives that are inclusive—and that doesn't mean wrapping himself in the Confederate flag.

During the Reagan-Bush era (1981-93), the CIA regularly rigged elections throughout the Third World, as in Nicaragua and El Salvador. There's a name political scientists use for these staged elections to create legitimacy: "demonstration elections." In Florida, the Bushes just showed us how to stage a demonstration election in the oldest democracy in the world.

BACK TO THE GOOD OLD DAYS

President-select George W. Bush's nomination of former Missouri Senator John Ashcroft as Attorney General is a major coup for the radical right and white supremacists. NAACP Board Chairman Julian Bond said of the choice, "Any pretense of unifying the nation has ended with this nomination. This confirms the correctness of blacks voting nine-to-one against Governor Bush."

Bush's selection is a logical one for a presidential candidate who refused to speak out against the Confederate flag flying over the South Carolina Statehouse during that state's primary. Our next president told us it was simply a question of "states' rights."

As it was a question of individual morality when Bush spoke at Bob Jones University, a Pentecostal college most famous for quoting the Bible to justify its practice of apartheid. Ashcroft received an honorary doctorate from Bob Jones in 1999, a university renowned for its racist policies and bigoted denunciation of the Catholic and Mormon churches.

As the nominee for the highest law enforcement position in the United States, Ashcroft has pledged "to be a guardian of liberty and equal justice." The key is understanding what he means by this.

In 1998, Ashcroft gave a revealing interview to the leading journal of the neo-Confederate movement, *Southern Partisan*. Ashcroft lauded the journal since it "helps set the record straight" on the Civil War by "defending Southern patriots" like Robert E. Lee, Stonewall Jackson and Jefferson Davis. He feared without Confederate apologist publications, people would get the idea that his Southern heroes had a "perverted agenda."

Ashcroft no doubt thanks his version of a bigoted and racist God for the *Partisan*'s ability to tell us fascinating tidbits, such as that slave owners "encouraged strong slave families to further the slave's peace and happiness." The journal was also one of the first publications to portray former Klan leader David Duke as "a populist spokesperson for a recapturing of the American ideal."

As usual, the foreign press covered the Ashcroft nomination far more accurately than the U.S. media. Note the headline in the December 23 *Independent of London*: "Bush Selects Right-Winger As Law Chief." The British paper remarked matter-of-factly, "Mr. Ashcroft can be expected to take the Justice Department sharply to the right." So much for Bush understanding that he lost the popular election by more than 500,000 votes.

Ashcroft is the son of a Pentecostal preacher who moved his family to Springfield, Missouri, so they could be close to the Assembly of God church headquarters. One of his favorite quotes is that there's only "two things you find in the middle of the road, a moderate and a dead skunk." That's why Phyllis Schlafly's Eagle Forum gave Ashcroft a 100-percent rating last year before he lost to a dead man, Governor Mel Carnahan, in his Senate re-election bid.

Right-wing religious zealot Cal Thomas offers an extensive interview with Ashcroft in his book, *Blinded by Might: Can the Religious Right Save America?* From what, you might ask. "Moral decline," of course.

Ashcroft yearns for the good old days, when women were ladies and blacks were Negroes. Ashcroft told Thomas that the decline of America, "this reversal in value flow, I think, can be clearly traced to the Great Society era." During this devilish period, the Kennedy-Johnson War on Poverty caused poverty to fall from 22 percent of the population in 1960 to 11 percent by 1966. A variety of Satanic programs were put in place, like Head Start for disadvantaged children, the Civil Rights Act of 1964 mandating equal rights for women and blacks in hiring and promotion, and the Voting Rights Act of 1965 which guaranteed every U.S. citizen—until the Bush brothers' Florida debacle—the right to vote.

Ashcroft has his own version of the Great Society, it's called "charitable choice." Separation of church and state aside, under his plan, federal money should go directly to churches to save America's soul.

"Moral choices are primarily shaped by the culture, and culture shapes behavior in an anticipatory or preventative way," Ashcroft holds. That's why he's offended by any mention that George Washington was a slave owner. He dismisses this as "malicious attacks" and "revisionist nonsense." He loves Washington, the Southern slaveowner, but detests Washington, D.C., the black city.

The Reverend Jesse Jackson said, "He [Ashcroft] is a very real threat to the years of civil rights and social justice progress." Ashcroft is also fiercely anti-abortion.

Ashcroft opposed the confirmation of Bill Lann Lee as U.S. Assistant Attorney General for the Civil Rights Division because Lee was against California's Proposition 209, which eliminated affirmative action in that state.

Ashcroft scuttled the appointment of African-American Ronnie White as a federal judge, attacking White as "pro-criminal" while on the Missouri Supreme Court. White's great offenses: he only supported the death penalty in 41 out of 59 cases and he once challenged the legality of a Missouri police drug check point—a practice later declared unconstitutional by the U.S. Supreme Court.

If Ashcroft manages to squeak through, he'll owe Bush heavily. Maybe he can do the same kind of favor that Attorney General William French Smith did for the Reagan-Bush administration in 1982. You remember, CIA Director William J. Casey negotiated a secret "memorandum of understanding" with Smith, agreeing that the CIA was not legally responsible for reporting drug trafficking into the U.S. by CIA "assets."

THE SOUTH RISES AGAIN

C an that Bush boy pick 'em or what? First, there was former Senator "I Lost to a Dead Guy" John Ashcroft—armed with an honorary Ph.D. from Bob Jones University—for Attorney General. Now there's Gale Norton for Secretary of the Interior.

Bypassing the usual polite gibberish that masquerades as mainstream "journalism" in this country, let's turn quickly to the British press, where the *Observer of London* ran this headline on January 14: "Unrepentant South mounts new assault on Washington." Cutting to the heart of the matter, the *Observer* correctly noted: "At the core of both nominees' [Ashcroft and Norton] objections to the federal offices they now assume is their shared, openly declared admiration for the old Southern Confederacy—declarations which have themselves provoked outrage as each comes forward for nomination."

Ashcroft's a great fan of "Southern patriots" like Robert E. Lee and Jefferson Davis; Norton apparently shares these sentiments. Last week, President-select George W. Bush had to explain to the *New York Times* a speech Norton made in 1996.

Surely it would be unfair to quote Norton out of context or fail to put her speech in some personal political/historical perspective. You can find the speech at the Independence Institute's website where she's listed as one of the "Heroes of Devolution" (code word for states' rights).

Then the Attorney General of Colorado, Norton pumped up the audience in the opening of the 1996 speech by pointing out, "We'll have the opportunity to do battle once again on the issue of the state being able to make its own decision." She went on to list some hideous examples of federal government oppression: "the wheelchair ramp required by the Americans with Disabilities Act" at the Colorado State Capitol; "auto emissions" testing; the "Fair Labor Standards Act"; and, of course, the notorious "Violence Against Women Act (VAWA)."

Norton went so far as to suggest that there's no constitutional ground for the VAWA, conveniently ignoring the 14th Amendment's equal protection clause. She demanded that Congress quit meddling and "shift that power back to where it belongs," to the states.

In Norton's rigid ideology, the federal government is always bad and meddlesome whether it's protecting women from violence or ensuring overtime pay after eight hours of work in a day. On the other hand, all those who fight for "state sovereignty" are good.

Norton related an emotional revelation she had while tramping through a Civil War graveyard in Virginia: "I had just gone through this massive battle with the EPA on state sovereignty and states' rights," she said. "I remember seeing this column that was erected in one of those graveyards. It said in memory of all the Virginia soldiers who died in defense of the sovereignty of their state. It really took me aback. Sure, I had been filing briefs and I thought that was pretty brave... Again, we certainly had bad facts in that case [the Civil War] where we were defending state sovereignty by defending slavery. But we lost too much. We lost the idea that the states were to stand against the federal government gaining too much power over our lives. This is the point I think we need to re-appreciate."

Julian Bond, chair of the NAACP, chided Norton for "wanton insensitivity against slavery and its descendants."

Bush saw it differently. He told the *New York Times* that his Secretary of the Interior nominee "was talking about states' rights, the ability of states to run their business... She was in no way, shape or form embracing slavery, and neither was John Ashcroft." Bush and the Republican spinmeisters challenged reporters to look at his nominees' entire records.

Fair enough.

As Colorado's Attorney General, Norton's political record is a testament to the re-appreciation of states' rights. In 1993, Norton fought valiantly to preserve Colorado's first-in-the-nation anti-gay legislation. She argued and lost before the conservative U.S. Supreme Court that civil rights shouldn't apply to gay people. "Such safeguards apply only to 'traditional suspect classes,' such as racial minorities, while other 'identifiable groups' including homosexuals have no fundamental right to seek enactment of legislation to benefit them," Norton maintained, according to the *Cleveland Plain Dealer*.

In August 1995, Norton, ever an admirer of Alabama, called for Colorado to reinstate the chain gangs in order to "combine hard work with humiliation."

In the middle of a campaign for U.S. Senate, Norton also routinely denounced the evils of Occupational Safety and Health Administration laws, the *Denver Post* reported. After her loss in the 1996 Senate race (to a live candidate), she recovered quickly enough to issue a statewide legal opinion banning all race-based scholarships at Colorado State University. Denver's NAACP accused her of pandering "to the extremist anti-affirmative action crowd." She told Denver's *Rocky Mountain News*, "It is dangerous for the government to be categorizing people on the basis of race for any reason."

The next year, she emerged as a major spokesperson for the New Citizenship Project Council on Crime in America's reactionary report promoting massive incarceration. The *South Bend Tribune* summarized the study this way: "Americans face a frightening future in which teenage 'wolf packs' roam the streets, inner-city gangsters spread into the suburbs, and hardened criminals waltz out of the prisons to prey on innocents."

Some of the highlights of the council's study were the fact that jails and prisons worked and that a disproportionate number of crimes are committed by blacks in the United States, reflecting the sad state of African-American families.

Norton told the *Tribune*, "Any social group that does not have a predominance of stable families is going to have serious crime problems... Incarceration works." The report was issued amid a steady drop in crime and academic studies indicating that black family problems may be the direct result of over-incarceration of black males for nonviolent minor drug offenses.

Norton crusaded to end Medicaid-funded abortions for women impregnated by rape or incest and fought against the mainstreaming of the physically disabled as excessive federal interference. She, of course, favored allowing industrial polluters to police themselves. Norton's political mentor is former Secretary of the Interior James Watt, who said the goal of his department should be to utilize natural resources as quickly as possible before the imminent return of Jesus Christ. Utilizing the parable of the Talents, the Watt thesis held that Jesus would be really pissed off if he returned and found some redwoods still standing.

Let's turn to the Brits' *Observer* for a summary: "Both Ashcroft and Norton are figureheads in a revived, neo-Confederate movement which blends the libertarian, anti-Washington and 'anti-bureaucrat' message of the Bush campaign with more militant sentiments that flirt with the Confederate and militia movements on the extreme right wing that reject the very notion of federal authority over 'States' Rights'—the battle cry of the old South."

FITRAKIS

January 18, 2001

CAN THE GENERAL MAKE PEACE?

The unasked question about Colin Powell, nominated as Secretary of State by George W. Bush, is an obvious one: Why would you appoint the former head of the Joint Chiefs of Staff, a war-maker, as your chief diplomat, supposedly a negotiator in peace-making?

Perhaps the best single source for reflecting on Powell's career is the five-part series "Behind Colin Powell's Legend," published by the sterling investigative web site ConsortiumNews.com. The series traces the development of Powell mania following the publishing of a Horatio Alger-like tale in his mid-1990s autobiography *My American Journey*. On tour in 1995 to promote the book, Powell's preference for using the U.S. military as the global Robocop clearly came through. Powell liked to brag about the "superb performance of the armed forces of the United States in recent conflicts, beginning with the...Panama invasion and then through Desert Shield and Storm."

What Powell fails to address is why three-quarters of the nations in the United Nations voted to condemn the U.S. operation in Panama as a flagrant violation of international law. You remember Operation Just Cause, an illegal armed intrusion into Panama to serve a warrant on Panamanian Manuel Noriega, who had recently been on the CIA payroll. Given

President-select Bush's obvious inexperience in foreign policy, Powell's past performance is essential in understanding what we might expect from another Bush administration.

Both ConsortiumNews and *In These Times* have raised the issue of Powell's actions in Vietnam, where the general describes burning peasants out of their hut in 1963, "starting the blaze with Ronson and Zippo lighters."

Headquartered in the Americal division, Major Powell in 1968 was involved in whitewashing initial allegations that U.S. troops has committed atrocities against Vietnamese civilians. It's well-established in the public record that Tom Glen, a member of an Americal platoon, wrote to General Creighton Abrahms charging that "for mere pleasure, [U.S. soldiers] fire indiscriminately into Vietnamese homes and without provocation or justification shoot at the people themselves."

Powell, in a reoccurring pattern in his rise to power, declined to interview Glen, but instead went to the superior officer who claimed Glen had no actual knowledge of atrocities. As *In These Times* reminds us in an editorial, Powell concluded, "In direct refutation of [Glen's] portrayal, is the fact that relationships between American soldiers and the Vietnam people are excellent." Within seven months, uninvestigated Americal troops would slaughter 347 Vietnamese civilians, including infants, in the village of My Lai.

As a lieutenant colonel, Powell received a Richard Nixon White House fellowship, which allowed him to ally himself with Nixon aides Caspar Weinberger and Frank Carlucci. When Weinberger and Carlucci took over the Defense Department as Defense Secretary and Assistant Defense Secretary respectively, under Reagan, they had a friend in Colonel Powell at the Pentagon.

By 1983, Powell was a general. He emerged as Weinberger's gatekeeper at the Pentagon and a key operative in the cover-up of the notorious Iran-Contra scandal. In September 1983, Powell, Weinberger and a young Lieutenant Colonel Oliver North went on an inspection tour of Central America together where they met with the CIA's "man in Panama," Noriega, who had well-known ties to Colombia drug traffickers. In November 1983, the Defense Department hosted a Washington lunch honoring their ally, Noriega.

Carlucci went on to be Reagan's National Security Advisor and, by

December 1986, Powell became Deputy National Security Advisor—primarily, ConsortiumNews suggests, because "Powell had played a crucial role in skirting the Pentagon's stringent internal controls over missile shipments to get the weapons out of Defense warehouses and into the CIA pipeline."

Powell officially claims that he knew nothing about the illegal shipment of missiles to Iran prior to their formal authorization on January 17, 1986. Oliver North testified, however, that "my original point of contact was General Colin Powell, who was going directly to his immediate superior, Secretary Weinberger." Powell helped draft Reagan's infamous March 4, 1987, speech admitting that there'd been a simultaneous release of arms to the Iranians for hostages in violation of stated U.S. policy.

As the administration hung North out to dry as the "cowboy" fall guy, Powell lobbied journalists behind the scenes to limit the investigation. By the time Reagan left office, Powell was a four-star general.

On October 2, 1989, Powell became the Chair of the Joint Chiefs of Staff and, on December 17, recommended the massive invasion of Panama to serve a warrant on Noriega. While the U.S. Army was there, they managed to destroy the Panamanian Defense Force and install a pro-U.S. government. The independent documentary *Panama Deception* remains required viewing for those who want the truth about Powell and the Panama invasion.

Powell has already pledged to work with U.S. allies to sanction rogue regimes like Iraq, where more than 1.5 million civilians died due to the embargo in the 1990s, and he'll have his hands full with the continuing imbroglio in the Middle East. Will the former war-maker have the diplomatic tact needed to peacefully cool these volatile situations? Powell's legacy from My Lai to Iran-Contra to Panama suggests only a policy of secrecy, cover-ups and illegal military activities.

January 18, 2001

THE UNELECTED RESIDENT

t's official. The Banana Republicans now occupy the White House. In direct—and predictable—contradiction to his campaign rhetoric of accommodation and compromise, George W. Bush begins his illegitimate regime like countless other coup figureheads—with cynicism and an iron hand.

How firmly will the forces of democracy oppose him? Remember that Bush was allowed to take power precisely because the Democrats lack the strength or character to stand up to the hard right. Predictably, their performance at the dawn of the Shrub years is already discouraging.

Indeed, if American democracy is to survive at all, clear and powerful resistance must come from where it always comes—the grassroots—but with far more conviction than we've seen in many decades.

The clearest sign of the Bush hard line comes with his chief law enforcement officer. Attorney General nominee John Ashcroft is a carbon copy of countless martial strongmen installed in Third World countries by the father of the new President and the national security apparatus the elder Bush once ran. The former Missouri Senator (who was beaten for re-election by a dead man) is the creation of the corporations and fundamentalist church groups that paid for his losing campaign—and for that of his new boss.

Ashcroft is pro-corporation (especially tobacco), pro-gun, pro-military, pro-death penalty, pro-welfare for religious schools, and an ardent fan of the Confederacy. He is anti-black, anti-choice, anti-feminist, anti-gay, anti-speech, anti-poor, anti-green and anti-labor.

In short, he's a poster child for the Bush junta, a humorless gray cabal of old economy types whose primary agenda will be to further the Reaganite redistribution of wealth from the poor to the rich while raping the planet's natural resources along the way. They'll add billions in church and corporate welfare. In the name of "liberty," they'll erase as many individual rights and freedoms as the bought Supreme Court will allow.

Star wars is only the most visible of the massive military and other scams this militant right-wing crew intends to foist on the public in the coming years, to the benefit of their corporate and fundamentalist sponsors. We can also expect an escalated drug war, new jungle bloodshed in Central America, heightened tensions with China and Russia, and a relentless assault on the natural environment and basic freedoms of speech and the press. All are sure to come.

The regime has been pre-bought by more than $350 million in contributions made to the Bush campaign in a larger national "election" that cost some $3 billion, much of that paid to electronic media, whose opposition to campaign finance reform is thus guaranteed.

Alongside Ashcroft is Gale Norton as Bush's Secretary of Interior nominee. A fanatic "property rights" cultist, Norton says the public can't impose environmental or other restrictions on private property owners. Thus she opposes the Clean Air and Water Acts, the National Parks system and all other communal attempts to preserve the natural environment and other life support systems essential to our collective survival.

Norton's ideology got new swagger last week from the U.S. Supreme Court, which used a "states' rights" argument to vastly weaken the Clean Water Act in a case involving a landfill in northern Illinois. By the usual 5-4 margin, the right-wing majority said the federal government could not overrule the states to save a body of water, even though that natural entity is part of a larger national ecosystem. For pure hypocrisy, the Supreme Court ruling is hard to top. It's a reminder of who, exactly, is taking control of the White House—and how.

History will recall that in the election of 2000, George W. Bush lost the nationwide popular vote to Al Gore by some 539,947 votes, plus the uncounted thousands in Florida. Not to mention another 2.6 million votes that went to Green Party candidate Ralph Nader.

History will note that, in a dozen different ways, Bush almost certainly lost the popular vote in Florida. Had Bush's brother not been governor there, Gore would have won the state's electoral votes and the electoral college. Had Bush's cousin not been perched at Fox News—and was the first network election chief to call the state for Shrub—the other TV networks might not have followed suit and instead covered the race properly on election night.

History will further note that with its fraternal Republican Governor and a Republican Secretary of State that was Bush's campaign chair, the state of Florida waged a systematic and effective campaign to disenfranchise blacks and Jews who were known to be supporting Gore by margins of four-, five- and even nine-to-one.

Black citizens were removed from the voter rolls en masse by false charges that they were felons, a move choreographed by a sophisticated computer firm hired with state money to do just that. African-Americans were stopped from reaching the polls by police who demanded various forms of impossible identification. African-Americans were booted from actual voting stations by phony requirements reminiscent of the old poll taxes and other scams used by the descendants of John Ashcroft's beloved Confederacy. Voting machines in black and Jewish districts conveniently malfunctioned and made a mockery of democracy.

Only the old Soviet Joe Stalin could aptly describe the Florida outcome: "It doesn't matter who casts the votes, only who counts them."

To make sure those votes were counted for a Bush victory, the United States Supreme Court stepped in—first ruling that the Florida recounts must stop, then, three days later, ruling there was no time to resume the recount.

To justify its demand that George W. Bush win the election, the Court's conservative majority used a series of tortured and inconsistent arguments that essentially imposed federal control on the state's electoral process. The Supreme Court demanded, among other things, a uniform standard for counting ballots when no such a doctrine has ever existed in federal law. The court trashed the very states' rights philosophy so-called conservatives have used for two centuries as a cover to oppose federal guarantees of such inconvenient luxuries as civil rights, civil liberties, voting rights and environmental protection. In short, the federal imposition used to guarantee Bush's victory is in direct ideological contradiction to the states' rights arguments the same justices used to overturn the ecological protection of those waterways in Illinois.

Also lost in the shuffle were the justices' own conflicts of interest. Both Chief Justice William Rehnquist and Justice Sandra Day O'Connor had long since made public their desire to retire from the bench, along with their unwillingness to do so with a Democrat in the White House. The wife of Justice Clarence Thomas and the sons of Justice Antonin Scalia all had direct personal interests in a Bush victory based on jobs they held at the time of the decision. Scalia also made known his desire to become Chief Justice, which could only happen if Rehnquist resigned under a Republican president, such as George W. Bush.

The electoral debacle of the year 2000 thus forever bankrupted any residual credibility remaining to the conservatives' arguments for states' rights. From now on, decisions such as the Illinois wetlands destruction will be tagged with the footnote that the Court remained firm in its commitment to states' rights—except in cases involving the election of a Republican president to the White House. Other than his intellectual mediocrity and exceptional meanness of spirit, history will remember Rehnquist only for his signature theft of the 2000 election, and the permanent damage done to the Supreme Court's once-towering credibility as an incorruptible institution of last resort.

How will history remember George W. Bush? Liberal pundits expect a field day with Shrub's obvious lack of intellectual and oratorical firepower. His voluminous malapropisms already rival those of his father. Smug Democrats assume his lack of charisma and bandwidth will automatically render him an ineffective, one-term failure. Having inherited the family business, whenever a really tough decision comes along he'll call his father. Poppy's cabinet is his personal missile shield.

But one need only remember Ronald Reagan to recall the danger of underestimation. Liberals branded Reagan "an amiable dunce." But he was neither. Ronnie's most decidedly un-amiable programs were brutal to the poor, the environment, women, people of color, the people of Central America. His lack of bookish intellect did not stop him from charming the media and enough of the American public to enforce the most destructive social agenda since Calvin Coolidge. Though his popularity ratings were far below those of Bill Clinton, Reagan managed to run up the biggest financial, educational and ecological debt in national history and to imbue an entire generation with a deep-rooted sense of materialistic cynicism.

In short, Reagan's rightist accomplishments were staggering.

Can Shrub repeat? Those who assume his deer-in-the-headlights demeanor dooms him to failure might recall his debates with Al Gore, where the obviously brighter but terminally arrogant Vice President flashed his brittle core and lost an election that had been handed to him on a silver platter.

In so doing, Gore revealed the real black hole of the coming era—the Democrats. The signal moment came last week, when—despite howls of rage from the Congressional Black Caucus—not one of the 50 Senate Democrats could muster the common decency to force a public debate over the most obviously stolen American election since 1876.

Eight years ago, when a legitimately elected Bill Clinton assumed office, Republican zealots waited nary a nanosecond to launch a full-scale partisan attack over everything from gays in the military to the new President's persona. For two full terms, conservatives waged an unrelenting assault on every particle of Clinton's moderate agenda, capping it off with a full-blown impeachment over his endlessly entertaining love life.

Clinton obliged by fighting hard for nothing except NAFTA and a wildly creative redefinition of what constitutes sex. The New Democratic agenda was a corporate-funded moderate Republican charade dressed in baby boomer blue-jeans.

The Clinton/Gore ticket proposed a feeble national healthcare plan, then tossed it at the first sign of corporate opposition. They dismantled the welfare system (for the poor, not the corporations) in ways no Republican could have dared. They compiled a truly horrendous record on civil liberties in general and wiretapping in particular. They escalated the drug war, jacking the U.S. prison population to a staggering two million while arguing to the U.S. Supreme Court, in the administration's dying days, that state referenda for medical marijuana should be overturned.

The Clinton administration did greatly aid the environment by vetoing, for eight years running, the nuclear power industry's attempt to flood the highways and railways with high-level radioactive waste headed to

Nevada. But they broke their promise to shut the WTI toxic waste incinerator in Eastern Ohio, which became a symbol for the administration's lack of green integrity and nerve.

Perhaps the most telling moment came in the Shrub debates, when the Texas oilman accused Gore of failing to implement an energy policy. The accusation could hardly have been more hypocritical—except that it was accurate.

For eight years, right into the Gore campaign, the administration talked a good game about fighting global warming and pushing renewable energy sources over fossil fuels. But their tangible accomplishments were marginal at best. They fudged on everything from auto efficiency standards to government purchases of recycled paper to utility deregulation to reactor safety. Clinton failed even to restore to the White House roof the solar panels installed by Jimmy Carter then removed by Reagan.

In the waning moments of his regime, with political costs lowest and exposure at its peak, Clinton indulged in a showy (but welcome) outburst of conservationism. His high-profile creation of millions of acres of national monuments, roadless wilderness and protected forests came like rain after an interminable drought.

But why at the end of his term, and not at the beginning? And why did he flinch from using the National Monuments Act to protect the Alaska Wildlife Refuge, soon to be pillaged by Shrub's hate-nature oil assault team?

Which brings us to the real reason the Democrats leave the White House with such an excruciatingly short list of tangible accomplishments: money. Bill Clinton's campaign genius has been to wed the hard realities of corporate cash with the slick gloss of social commitments. When push came to shove, he could always manage to ditch just enough of the social agenda to keep himself funded, but not too much to blow it with the public.

Al Gore's downfall was his inability to simultaneously dance to contradictory tunes. He raised so many millions that when George W. Bush astonishingly accused him of spending more on his campaign than the Republicans, Gore simply sighed and groaned, but had no comeback. For all his populist prattle, his soul was sold.

Because he couldn't double-dip like Clinton (and because he was too uptight to let Elvis campaign for him), Gore will (gratefully) fade into history along with Mike Dukakis and Walter Mondale. Clinton still runs the New Democratic Party. His brilliant celebrity wife will bide her time, learn the ropes, expand her base and, sooner or later, her time will come. And the Democrats will become ever more besotted with corporate money and the illusions of social justice.

But they will not stand up to the Bush junta. There have already been gutter fights over appointees like Linda Chavez and Gale Norton. But the heavy lifting, as usual, will be left to those outside the mainstream—in this case, those who supported Ralph Nader and the Green Party.

For years to come, the Democrats will scapegoat Nader for the 2000 election debacle. They will point to Nader's 90,000 votes in Florida and thousands more in New Hampshire as the deciding factor. They will ignore the fact—as they did last week in the U.S. Senate—that Gore actually won both the popular and the electoral vote. And that Nader had nothing to do with Bill Clinton's dalliance with Monica Lewinsky, or the spring crash of NASDAQ, or the untimely explosion of warfare in the Middle East, or the failure of Gore to carry his own state of Tennessee and Clinton's Arkansas (not to mention the Democratic stronghold of West Virginia), any one of which could have put Gore in the White House.

Nor did Nader cause Gore's pathetic showings in three debates (from which Nader was in fact physically removed), or Jeb Bush's theft of Florida, or the Supreme Court's cynical intervention. The Democrats will also suppress the fact that even though Gore was a miserable candidate who ran a miserable campaign, the election still had to be stolen by Bush, pure and simple.

Nonetheless, it will be convenient for the Democrats to point to every Shrub transgression as something that would not have happened had Ralph Nader not run for president. And then to do nothing about it.

Most important, the Democrats will forget the moment that Al Gore had the election wrapped up. At the Democratic National Convention in Los Angeles, Gore stole Nader's thunder and ignited the activist constituency. Gore gave the speech of his life, a straightforward populist call to action, perfectly designed to bring the truly committed back into the Democratic fold. In fact, Gore endorsed the agenda perfected over the past 35 years by none other than America's leading consumer activist.

Gore soared to a 15-point lead.

And then he wilted, as if his corporate sponsors panicked, and ripped up his roots. Gore gracelessly helped bar Nader from the debates, then lost them. Instead of co-opting the green agenda, Gore and his flunkies attacked the messenger.

We can expect the Democrats to fight the fringe battles over appointments and the like. But the only Americans who'll reliably resist the brunt of the Shrub assault are precisely those the Democrats trashed, along with those the Bush junta so methodically disenfranchised. The thousands of young and aging activists who paid to hear Nader rant. The 2.6 million who voted for him. The millions more who grudgingly voted for Gore but loathed his short-changed agenda and are ready to fight it out as the corporate aren't.

The same millions who expected a fair national hearing on how this election was stolen, and were denied it by a spineless Senate.

After the early skirmishes, and except for the easy battles, the Democrats will roll over for the Bush junta. Their money comes from the same corporations. They won't withstand a focused, massively financed right-wing juggernaut intent on substituting raw muscle for the lack of a popular mandate.

That's the way they do it in the Third World. Who will stop them here?

BUSH-WHACKED BY THE COURT

While his Fraudulence George W. Bush continues to masquerade as U.S. President—proposing that one percent of the wealthiest Americans get 42 percent of the tax cut—facts are flooding in documenting an Al Gore victory in Florida.

Ongoing investigations into Florida's 180,000 undercounted ballots document the predictable: The votes were intended for Gore. In an analysis by the *Chicago Tribune* and *Orlando Sentinel,* Gore picked up at least an additional 366 votes that were clearly marked, but discarded in rural Republican counties. Apparently, Republican county officials had a hard time discerning the voter's intent, as prescribed by Florida law, when one voter wrote the word "Gore" in the write-in slot.

The preliminary analysis by the *Washington Post* and the *Miami Herald* in eight counties, four of which went to Bush, indicate that Gore was preferred on 46,000 undercounted ballots, while Bush was preferred on only 17,000.

As the newspapers continue to tabulate the overwhelming Gore victory in Florida, other disturbing evidence reveals the extent of the Bush hoax. As this column reported just after the election, the Republican-connected ChoicePoint electronic data firm, hired through the office of Republican

Secretary of State Katherine Harris, "erroneously" eliminated 8,000 Florida voters on the grounds that they were felons. Since then, the *Albion Monitor* and other news sources have reported that Harris and ChoicePoint misidentified an additional 15 percent of voters in 10 Florida counties as felons, who also lost their right to vote. Fifty-four percent of those on the Hillsborough County ChoicePoint list were black. This is not a big surprise, since 93 percent of African-Americans nationwide voted for Gore.

Harris and ChoicePoint further shrunk the Democratic voter base by including on the felon list an additional 1,704 names of Florida residents who had been convicted of felonies in Ohio and Illinois—two states that restore citizenship and voting rights to people after they have served their time in prison. While only 13 states in the nation decline to restore voting privileges to felons, the vast majority of these are in the deep South, heart of the old Confederacy.

Adding to Bush's problem is the growing attack by law professors on the Supreme Court's 5-4 *Bush v. Gore* decision that stopped the Florida recount just as Gore was pulling ahead. On December 14, 2000, 280 law professors issued a statement charging that "The five justices were acting as political proponents for candidate Bush, not as judges."

"By stopping the recount in the middle, the five justices acted to suppress the facts. Judge Scalia argued that the justices had to interfere even before the Supreme Court heard the Bush team's argument because the recount might 'cast a cloud upon what [Bush] claims to be the legitimacy of his election,'" the law professors asserted. "Suppressing the facts to make the Bush government seem more legitimate is the job of propagandists, not judges."

The statement concludes: "By taking power from the voters, the Supreme Court has tarnished its own legitimacy. As teachers whose lives have been dedicated to the rule of law, we protest."

By January 9, 2001, 554 law professors from 120 law schools signed the statement in a full-page *New York Times* ad. As of February 1, the number had risen to 660.

Increasingly, legal scholars are suggesting that Chief Justice William Rehnquist devised a classic Catch-22 to defeat Gore. First, the Supreme Court ruled that the voting standards in Florida could not be changed and made clearer after the election, because that would constitute a "new law," which violates a federal statute. Then, in their second decision, the

Supreme Court halted the recount because the voting standards were not clear and violated constitutional guarantees of "equal protection," because the votes would be counted under different standards in different counties.

Conveniently, the court neglected to find that not counting a vote at all, when the intention of the voter was clear, also violates "equal protection" or a fundamental right. Thus, not counting votes is not only OK, but apparently constitutional, particularly in black and poor Democratic districts. Counting votes in slightly different ways from county to county—which is necessitated by the reality of different voting machines—is a violation of the Constitution.

Equally bizarre is the Supreme Court majority's insistence that they had to intervene because of an old federal law that gives "safe harbor" to electoral college members, guaranteeing that they can't be challenged if selected by December 12. The real reason they used the excuse of the December 12 date was to end the Florida recount before Gore pulled ahead.

Instead of looking to an old federal law, Rehnquist plus his Gang of Four might have consulted the 12th and 20th Amendments to the Constitution, where no such fetish with obscure dates exists: "The terms of President and Vice-President shall end at noon on the 20th day of January...and the Congress may by law provide for the case wherein neither a President-elect nor a Vice-President-elect shall have qualified, declaring who shall then act as President, or the manner in which one who is to act shall be selected, and such person shall act accordingly until a President or Vice-President shall have qualified."

The Constitution is much more concerned with electing a legitimate President, and not rushing to judgment. Rehnquist's five-justice majority prefers the role of propagandists, with Rehnquist as the great and powerful Oz in a black robe.

THE JUNTA TIGHTENS ITS GRIP

Anyone with a lingering soft spot for the "compassionate conservatism" of George W. Bush had best face some clear realities: This is a cynical, heartless junta, and our basic liberties—not to mention the planet's natural resources and a whole lot more—are in serious jeopardy.

Let's start with the war on drugs—or, more accurately, the war on civil liberties and black voters. Well beyond those few hundred disputed south Florida votes that the Supreme Court did not want recounted, the Jeb Bush administration is now known to have conducted an extremely sophisticated assault on African-Americans who dared go to the polls in 2000. Many were harassed and turned away from voting in ways not seen since the bad old days of Jim Crow. (Similar tactics were used in Tennessee, which Shrub carried by a very narrow margin, and other key Southern states.)

But the most effective tool to disenfranchise a population group that went 90 percent for Al Gore was the use of felony convictions, real and imagined. Under Florida law (and that of many other states) convicted felons lose their right to vote. Prior to the 2000 election, brother Jeb sent threatening letters to thousands of black Floridians who were not convicted felons telling them they were, and that they were therefore not eligible to vote. Some who showed up at the polls with evidence to the contrary were nonetheless informed they couldn't cast a ballot.

Meanwhile, tens of thousands of black citizens who had been thrown in jail were denied their voting rights under cover of law. A very high percentage were casualties of the drug war, raging now for some 30 years, since the glory days of Richard Nixon, but prosecuted with extreme stupidity and cupidity by Bill Clinton and Al Gore.

The war on drugs is, of course, a complete misnomer. It's focused not on the trillion-dollar-plus prescription and over-the-counter drug industry or on those highly addictive mass killers, alcohol and tobacco.

Instead it targets herb-based products like marijuana and cocaine, and psychedelics and other chemicals that somehow smack of the 1960s, or that threaten the profits of the real drug companies, especially the alcohol and tobacco industries. This multi-billion-dollar social assault has spawned a huge constituency of judges, lawyers, prison-builders and adventurers with a major stake in preserving its endless futility.

But in the wake of the 2000 election, it now serves another obvious function—guaranteeing the re-election of Republican candidates, prime among them George W. Bush.

The Clinton administration, of course, kept the fire going. In an act of staggering betrayal, they sent federal marshals into California to assault doctors who dared act in compliance with the voters' official approval of medical marijuana. A half-dozen other states have also approved such referenda. But Clinton left office with his federal attorneys demanding that the U.S. Supreme Court deny the legality of medical marijuana despite those popular votes.

Aside from the unspeakable hypocrisy of the argument, Clinton's escalation of the war on drugs, and his role in raising the U.S. prison population to two million citizens, were clearly among the many factors that cost Al Gore the White House. The Democrats simply handed the Bush boys the ultimate club to keep black voters away from the polls.

Don't think the lesson was lost on them. There were those who thought the Shrub might actually take a new tack on the drug war. It's a Republican governor (New Mexico's Gary Johnson) who's the highest-ranking proponent of legal marijuana. And the cost of the war continues to escalate for an administration some thought might actually care about saving taxpayer money.

But the Republicans aren't stupid. An escalated drug war means thousands more disenfranchised people of color, whose community continues to vote overwhelmingly Democratic—if, that is, they're allowed to vote at all, as they were not in Florida. A President who was selected by the Supreme Court, but who lost the popular election by 500,000 votes, is not about to throw away a tool like this.

So expect an escalation of the drug war, with an ever-higher percentage of non-white victims who are the core business of a booming prison industry that pumps billions into the pockets of Republican stalwarts.

Expect also an escalated assault on civil liberties. Like Pinochet in Chile and Somoza in Nicaragua, George W. Bush heads an unelected junta. The severest threat to any such regime is the right of people to organize, and be informed.

As documented by Anthony Lewis of the *New York Times*, among others, Bill Clinton's record on civil liberties was beyond horrendous. But Shrub can be expected to go even further. With the drug war, contrived foreign crises, and whatever else as pretext, this administration is certain to go after our basic rights with a vengeance. As its poll ratings plummet, it must be profoundly and accurately concerned that people who can organize and inform themselves are the ultimate threat to its hold on power.

Republicans have always talked about "getting government off our backs." But they're referring primarily to getting it off the backs of the big corporations that pay their way. When it comes to the rights of individual citizens, Republicans are first in line to slash away at freedom of speech, the press, protests against corporate abuses, a woman's right to choose, the First and Fourth Amendments, and those other inconveniences that form the bulwark of a true democracy.

What we now must realize is that an unelected President like this one can't tolerate a public with real power. And that we are going to have to work far harder to sustain even the semblance of a working democracy as long as this administration holds the White House.

MEDIA-MANUFACTURED LEGITIMACY

By now most readers are familiar with the misleading banner head-lines proclaiming George W. Bush the winner of the popular vote in Florida after a media recount. *USA Today*, a partner with the *Miami Herald* in the recount effort, dutifully ran the headline above the fold on April 4, as did local dailies across the nation.

The oft-cited and incredibly propagandistic *Herald* story also appeared on April 4, 2001. In order to manufacture a victory for Bush, the paper had to first subtract Gore's known previous gains in four counties—Palm Beach, Broward, Volusia and Miami-Dade. After the election, but before the Florida Supreme Court's ruling, some of the uncounted votes had been tabulated in those four counties, adding hundreds of votes to Gore. Then the Florida Supreme Court ruled that all of the state's uncounted votes must be counted. The blatant political intervention by the U.S. Supreme Court ended the Florida recount.

The *Herald/USA Today* spin is that if all the votes in the state had been counted under the Florida Supreme Court ruling, Bush would have still won. But all of those hundreds of documented but uncertified Gore votes in the four counties were thrown out of the newspapers' investigation, based on the *Herald/USA Today*'s assumption that they couldn't be included.

One day after the Orwellian headlines roared across America, the *Miami Herald*, with little fanfare, published a story saying that Gore would have won under a "clear intent of the voters" standard. How did the paper come to the opposite conclusion? Duh. They counted the uncounted votes, or "undervote," in all 67 counties. Hence, the little-referenced second-day story had Gore picking up an additional 1,475 votes in Palm Beach County and 1,081 more in Broward County.

As the investigative website ConsortiumNews.com points out: "Wednesday's misleading 'Bush won' story—pushed by the *Herald* and its recount partner *USA Today*—was widely embraced by the national press corps and applauded by Bush partisans in the White House. The new *Herald* story, entitled 'Recounts could have given Gore the edge,' received only a fraction of the national attention."

In a related bizarre twist, the *New York Times* reported that hundreds of uncounted ballots in Florida disappeared before the newspapers could count them. "In Orange County, for example, officials reported in November that they had found 966 ballots with no discernable vote for President," the *Times* noted on April 5. When the newspapers went back to discern the vote, 327 uncounted ballots were missing.

With even less fanfare, the third story in the *Herald* series found "a net gain of at least 210 votes for Gore in Orange and St. Lucia County, where optical scanners were used."

The *Herald/USA Today* investigation also found that in majority African-American precincts, where the vote went more than 90 percent for Gore, 8.9 percent of votes were uncounted, compared to 2.4 percent uncounted votes in majority white precincts.

The structure and conclusion of the *Herald/USA Today* series strongly suggests that they came to the conclusion that it was best for the country to believe that "Bush wins," even if it's supported only by the strangest hypothetical assumptions. By not counting the Gore votes in the four counties and then dribbling out information about the additional Gore votes, the papers effectively created a stampede that the national mainstream press willingly followed. Thus, a misleading interpretation has now become conventional wisdom, which will be routinely repeated by pompous journalists and right-wing talk show hosts. Big Brother would be proud.

WHAT DO WE CALL THE ASTERISK IN THE WHITE HOUSE?

America has a problem. For the first time in more than a century (with the exception of Gerald Ford), the White House is occupied by someone who did not win a national election. So we need a contest to find an accurate title for him.

President doesn't cut it. George W. Bush lost the general election to Al Gore by more than 500,000 votes, not counting the 2.6 million that went to Ralph Nader, and still more for Pat Buchanan and others.

Gerry Ford, as you may recall, became president after Richard Nixon resigned. So Ford became the Oaf of Office without even running in a national election.

But we called him President anyway because it was a short term he had to fill, from Nagasaki Day in 1974 through the 1976 election. He wasn't the brightest bulb ever to light up the Oval Office, but it was understood his filler time was brief before the public would either say yea or nay to a full term. And, besides, he was a pretty nice guy, even if he'd played foot-ball without wearing a helmet. Whatever his faults, Ford was an aptly named All-American.

George W. Bush is a different story entirely. Polls now show fully 20 percent of the American public—some 50 million people or more—believe he (and his brother, along with assorted other relatives at Fox News and elsewhere) stole the 2000 election. That's a big, angry number that's not about to go down. Many of those who hold that belief also argue that outright racism and likely anti-Semitism were involved.

Another 30 percent believe that Bush did not legitimately win the election, i.e. they think he may not have stolen it, but that he certainly came in second. Given the actual numerical results, it's a belief that's more than understandable.

That leaves us with half the country holding, at very best, a highly tenuous acceptance or willingness to follow the man who claims to be our national leader. This does not make for a nation in which consensus on the true title of the man claiming to be President will come easily.

Unfortunately, this does not appear to hold true for the Supreme Corporate Army of Bombastic Bloviators (SCABB), which dominates the major media, from Fox and the networks to the op-ed pages and mainstream talk radio. From George Will to Rush Limbaugh, from Tom Friedman to Cokey Roberts, the smug, arrogant and thoroughly bought pontificators who pollute the people's airspace have taken to groveling at Bush's feet as if he had an actual IQ.

"Beating everyone's expectations" is the quip of the day, as if the fact that El Jefe can occasionally speak a complete sentence and has not (yet!) gotten us into a nuclear war makes him equivalent to the second coming of Franklin Roosevelt.

Those who can wade through the horrendous toxic manure pile of hype and hysteria about the first hundred days of the junta's hold on American power without a deep sense of nausea and vertigo are now being counted by pollsters as firm evidence that the Republicans are headed toward a new national consensus.

Hardly. Part of the problem: We don't know what to call this guy. He has no legitimate title. He is not, rightfully, the President. And he hardly even has a name of his own.

A number of publications, most notably *The Nation*, have carried out contests to come up with an adequate title for the current, shall we say, Pretender. Many suggestions were filed. The winner was apparently an abbreviated version of one that appeared in this column immediately after the stolen election. We called Bush the Unelected Resident. *The Nation* has apparently settled on just Resident.

The esteemed Molly Ivins, perhaps the only nationally syndicated columnist with both a social conscience and a sense of humor, has called Bush both Shrub and Dubya. These, however, are family names, and don't really qualify as official titles.

Other publications have resorted to other monikers. His Fraudulency, for example. But that one is more apropos to historical journals, as it was previously tacked onto Rutherford B. Hayes, who took the White House via the stolen election of 1876. Just as future historians are certain to view the campaign of 2000, no serious historian disputes that the 1876 contest was stolen. And 1876 had as devastating an impact on the former slave community of the American South as Shrub's taking of the White House is likely to have on the global ecology.

Those who think in terms of soft drinks have labeled him the unPresident. Other popular journalistic vehicles include pResident, and using quotation marks, as in "President." Then, in recognition of Roger Maris, some are using President*. The asterisk is meant to recall the year 1961, when Maris hit 61 home runs, breaking Babe Ruth's record of 60 but doing so in 162 games, instead of the 154 it took Ruth.

Many Americans thought Maris was no more the home run king than Bush is the president. But Maris retired quietly and ran a beer business later in life. He never threatened to get the United States into a war with China based in part on his oblivious misstatements on a TV talk show.

Bush's SCABB apologists have since argued that it was early, and George II really can't be held accountable for everything he says, and that he stopped drinking beer when he was 40, 10 years after he was arrested for drunk driving.

They also whine that this first 100 days have really changed our view of the man. And they're right.

During the campaign, we thought he was, well, dumb. Canny, maybe, but not really too smart. Now there's no room for doubt on either account.

We thought he might attempt to rape and pillage the planet on behalf of the corporations that own him, most importantly the oil, gas, coal and nuke industries. Since the public didn't elect him, but rather he was installed by big polluting interests, we feared he might put his sponsors' profits ahead of the public good. Now there's absolutely not a shred of doubt.

We thought also his foreign policy view of the world, and particularly of China, might be somehow locked down in the Cold War, somewhere around 1961, when Maris hit those 61* home runs. Now we know his psyche is stuck somewhere around 1952, when we were at war in Korea, whose leadership—both North and South—he has just thoroughly insulted and provoked. "I shall return," promised the Commie-hating General Douglas MacArthur, but who would've guessed the Old Warrior would be reincarnated as the son of George H.W. Bush?

Bush the Younger is also being compared to Herbert Hoover, the Republican who presided over the onset of the Great Depression. This is blatantly unfair—to Hoover. The Iowa engineer was in fact a competent and resourceful administrator whose policies in some positive ways foreshadowed the New Deal, even if his callous attitude toward the poor rightfully landed him in the historic doghouse. Suffice it to say there is not one member of the Bush cabinet that could stand next to Hoover in terms of pure intelligence and competence.

None of this, of course, means Dubya is to be underestimated. Quite the opposite. Whatever we wish to call him, George W. Bush has absolutely clarified his limitless ability to butcher not only the English language, but the very fabric of our social structure, our financial well-being and our ability to survive on this planet.

But as George Orwell understood all too well, language is powerful. Those who control it control both the present and the future. So the SCABB pontificators need a counter-balance, and the Shrub needs a title. Send your suggestions in now, care of this newspaper.

We're in desperate need of new language to deal with a very old phenomenon: a coup d'etat by the mean-spirited, the incompetent, the thoroughly corrupt, and the very dangerous.

Update: Many of the suggestions we received from readers were profoundly disrespectful and cannot be printed in a family publication. Some leaned to the esoteric and obscure, such as "Beer Hall Putz" and "FACE." Two seemed like word games: "Bu(ll)sh(it)" and "PuResident." There have also been "George II" and "pResident."

But I dedicate my next pint of Ben & Jerry's to my personal favorite: "President Quayle."

BEHOLD THE BURNING SHRUB

The Old Testament says Moses saw a burning bush. Today it's our planet that's on fire, and the Bush administration is pouring on the gas. The official assault on solar, wind, efficiency and conservation is an ungodly call to global suicide.

The Burn-the-Planet Energy Plan is based on escalated addictions to fossil and radioactive fuels that are economically and ecologically obsolete. The administration is a desperate huckster, peddling outdated inventory before new technology makes it unsaleable. Despite some green window trim, this plan turns back the clock 50 years, and threatens our ecological and economic survival.

It attacks natural alternatives poised to guarantee a clean, cheap, reliable, safe, virtually infinite supply. But it maximizes profits for the oil, coal, gas and nuclear multi-nationals that have made George W. Bush and Dick Cheney rich, and that help sustain the Republican Party.

Let's start from the bottom. The mining and burning of coal is an economic, health and ecological disaster. Strip mining and mountain-top removal, as practiced in West Virginia and elsewhere, is an irreversible ecological catastrophe with devastating long-term economic impacts. It degrades virgin land into lethal moonscapes. The particulate and other emissions from coal—including significant radioactivity—cost us billions yearly in cancer, asthma, heart and lung problems and other health disasters, both for those who mine it and all of us who breathe. Coal is a huge contributor to global warming, acid rain and a host of other eco-disasters.

As is oil. Accelerated drilling and burning of oil adds spills, emissions, and assaults on public health to its acceleration of global warming. Cheney says oil's opponents somehow deny "21st-century" technologies. But the Alaskan ecosystem has yet to recover from the *Exxon Valdez*, and the rest of the planet suffers from daily spills that are neither better nor, ultimately, any smaller.

Any true "21st-century" energy plan would include an end to oil. Virtually none of it is used to generate electricity. And virtually all our increased use has stemmed from government failures to mandate more efficient cars, buildings or other wasters of fuel. The administration would slash and burn programs meant to make further drilling unnecessary. The right to drive SUVs and to deny the public mass transit is being exalted above the right to breathe clean air and protect our global life support systems.

Ditto atomic energy. After 50 years and trillions of dollars invested, U.S. nukes provide less than 20 percent of our electricity. They do it unreliably, dangerously and at phenomenal cost. Huge quantities of global-warming carbon dioxide are released at every step of the mining, processing, enrichment and burning of radioactive fuel. Radioactive waste management, on-going radioactive emissions and the probability of future disasters are just a few of the other problems that remain unsolved after a half-century of unlimited expenditure.

The most ardent nukesters admit no new reactors can come on line for at least five years. On February 3, 2001, in the shadow of Chernobyl and Three Mile Island, San Onofre Unit Three suffered a major fire, knocking out fully 25 percent of California's nuclear capacity. In May, a truck disaster killed two people and may have spilled radioactive materials on a Canadian highway, making it clear what's certain to happen if high-level wastes begin to move to some central dumping ground.

From the promise of electricity "too cheap to meter," nukes have become the ultimate indicator that the Burn-the-Planet Energy Plan has no future.

So what does work? Natural gas has an interim role to play—as a bridging fuel to hydrogen. Mining natural gas is dirty, moving it is expensive and wasteful, and burning it contributes to global warming. But as the least bad of the fossil fuels, methane will be with us for a while. Its use needs to be acknowledged, but any expansion needs to be carefully limited.

Methane can be biologically produced. But perhaps its most important feature is that its infrastructure could ultimately support the one movable fuel that makes long-term sense—hydrogen. Combining this single proton with oxygen produces energy and a single by-product—water. In fuel cells and other devices, it could prove the ideal fuel. Its production can and will be done cleanly and naturally.

Wind will be among the fuels producing it. Windpower is now the cheapest and fastest-growing new form of generation outside brown coal. It has no key role in the Burn-the-Planet Energy Plan. But industrial windmills are now key to the energy future of industrial Europe. The Minnesota Public Utilities Commission has deemed it the "least cost" alternative, and ordered at least 300 new megawatts to be built.

With virtually infinite wind capacity between the Mississippi and the Rockies—a "Saudi Arabia of wind" that includes Texas—any sane energy policy would focus on vast new investments in turbines that can also save thousands of struggling family farms with lease payments.

Similar breakthroughs are here with solar power. Photovoltaic cells, which convert sunlight to electricity, have plummeted in price, and will go down even further as production ramps up. They are cheaper than nukes, and can be installed on rooftops throughout the industrialized world, helping to eventually make the electric grid obsolete. Next to wind, solar is the second-fastest growing new source of energy.

There are others in the natural camp—tidal power, ocean thermal, geothermal, bio-fuels, flywheels, hybrid cars—that are cheaper, clean, safer and more reliable than what the Burn-the-Planet Plan demands. Municipal ownership and decentralization, using photovoltaic cells, fuel cells, microturbines and other 21st-century devices, can help build true "energy independence." Consumers can free themselves from the grip of price-gouging utilities and suppliers (and the corporations behind the Bush administration).

There's also increased efficiency and conservation. America's energy system assumed infinite supply. It is wasteful, dirty, expensive and obsolete. As much as 50 percent savings can come merely from tightening up.

All this is clearly too much for two men still working for the oil industry.

Cheney and Bush's Burn-the-Planet Energy Plan is a holdover from a bygone millennium. Gouge and pollute were the order of the day. All that mattered were fossil and nuke profits. The Cheney-Bush plan exalts cynicism, greed and intentional obsolescence. Its day is done.

The renewable/efficiency/conservation "green alternative" is clean, cheap, reliable—and necessary. Forget the Texas oilmen's "real men don't conserve" sneers. We have an available and necessary energy vehicle to guarantee our economic stability and ecological survival.

The burning Bush says push has come to shove. And the choice is between death or life.

RIGHT
MAKES
MIGHT

I had an opportunity last week to attend a lecture by one of my favorite writers and researchers, Chip Berlet, senior analyst at Political Research Associates. His new book, co-written with historian Matthew Lyons, titled *Right-Wing Populism in America: Too Close For Comfort* (Guilford Press), is an essential guide for sorting out the political octopus we call the "right" in the United States.

Berlet and Lyons, in their thick tome, ask a critical question: Why can such blatantly anti-democratic political forces thrive in our country? While the mainstream media briefly focused on the rise of right-wing militias and other anti-federal groups after the Oklahoma City bombing, the press conspicuously avoided Timothy McVeigh's neo-Nazi sentiments prior to his recent execution.

Berlet and Lyons document how McVeigh "moved from conspiracist anti-government beliefs into neo-Nazi ideology" before he blew up the Oklahoma City federal building on April 19, 1995. McVeigh's affection for neo-Nazi William Pierce's *The Turner Diaries* is well known. What Berlet and Lyons managed to do is place that primer for a race war within "its central apocalyptic theme, the cleansing nature of ritual violence—a theme reminiscent of German Nazi ideology, which also sought a millenarian Thousand-Year Reich."

In his lecture, Berlet warned that it's too easy and incorrect to dismiss McVeigh as insane. The tendency to disparage McVeigh and his ilk as a lunatic fringe creates a political atmosphere that allows the FBI and other law enforcement agencies to repress the democratic left as well as the anti-democratic right. It also tends to ignore the values often espoused in main-stream politics and culture by the right that are similar to McVeigh's.

Berlet and Lyons argue that a powerful combination of anti-elitist rhet-oric, conspiracy theories and ethnic scapegoating propels myriad right-wing movements. And it's been this way throughout U.S. history. They spell out, in an insightful chart, a long-standing "Proceduralist narrative used in repressive right-wing populism." In layman's terms, they suggest that right-wing populists create a caricature of "elite parasites." (The fact that our current President fits this category so nicely is unfortunate.)

So the right-wing populists direct their anger toward these—you name them—"secret elites," "insiders," "international bankers," "liberal secular humanists," "government bureaucrats," "globalists," "Freemasons," "Illuminati" or Jews. But these enemies, mostly imagined, cause the right-wingers not to attack visible corporate power in the U.S.; while they are angry at the people at the top, they take their anger out on the people at the bottom. They turn their scapegoating and repressive and destructive actions against the poorest and most powerless. Why do they go after wel-fare mothers, blacks, immigrants and gays rather than real corporate wel-fare mothers with their tax abatements and subsidies?

Part of the answer is that it's the path of least resistance; the same rea-son water flows downhill. Another part of the answer is that progressive activists have not developed essential ground rules for countering right-wing populists.

Berlet forcefully argues that right-wing populism is driven by real, not imaginary, economic grievances. He stresses that it's important for the left to allow the right "an absolute right to seek redress of their grievances." It's a mistake to rely on the corporate-dominated state to limit the free speech rights of racists, sexists or homophobes. Ultimately, that just reinforces the right-wing's paranoia and conspiracy theories.

He also suggests that the progressive community has to do a much bet-ter job of distinguishing between right-wing leadership and their fol-lowers. Research often shows that followers are ill-informed and aren't drawn to a group because of its anti-democratic ideology but because they are "angry."

While it's important to criticize and counter the arguments of right-wing leaders, Berlet points out that it's equally important to listen to the grievances of their followers and not assume they are "sophisticated political agents."

Berlet believes that progressives have often been sloppy in refuting right-wing populism and resorted to simple anti-right slogans. This does little to counter the right's rhetoric that's often couched in American cultural imagery. Calling right-wing populists "racist, sexist bigots" doesn't refute their beliefs that affirmative action plans allow women and blacks to take their jobs away or that gays are out to establish "special rights" for themselves.

Part of this nonsense is actually fed to them by mainstream Republican politicians through orchestrated strategies and campaigns, from Richard Nixon's "Southern strategy," where he denounced "the Northeastern liberal elite," and Ronald Reagan's opening of his 1980 campaign in New Philadelphia, Mississippi, birthplace of the modern Ku Klux Klan, to Bush Senior's Willie Horton commercial and Bush Junior's wrapping himself in the Confederate flag during the South Carolina primary.

Berlet argues that progressives must build the broadest possible coalition in seeking to advance human rights and social justice. Recently he wrote, "Don't let your critics or establishment figures divide your coalition by targeting people or groups with unpopular ideas. The following familiar refrain is old and tired: If only your group didn't include [fill in the blank: anarchists, communists, feminists, gays and lesbians, vegans, witches, atheists] you would be more effective. Baloney. It's a trick. Allow one slice and the blade of division keeps cutting. Set your group's principles of unity in a democratic fashion and then welcome as participants all who abide by those rules."

FITRAKIS

July 5, 2001

NONE DARE CALL IT A CONSPIRACY

T he U.S. Commission on Civil Rights' recently published report on the Florida election debacle was widely portrayed as a pro-Gore political document. The Commission's conclusions that the Florida election results represented "injustice, ineptitude and inefficiency" are factually based and in line with a variety of news reports that have dribbled out separately and without much fanfare.

The Commission's report that 54 percent of the rejected ballots in Florida were cast by black voters has profound implications. Simple math reveals that black voters—who voted for Gore by 90 percent—were 10 times as likely as whites to have their votes voided. The report specifically singled out Governor Jeb Bush and his close friend and Republican ally Secretary of State Katherine Harris for blame.

Still, the Commission's reputed "political" report could find no "conclusive evidence" that the President's brother and his top appointed officials "conspired" to deny voting rights for black voters, although the Commission suggested the U.S. Justice Department might want to investigate.

The Justice Department should start with the so-called "felon list" controversy. Greg Palast of the BBC initially reported that a large number of non-felons in Florida were denied their constitutional right to vote because their names appeared on a felon list.

In a two-part series running May 31 and June 1, 2001, the *Washington Post* similarly concluded that "hundreds, perhaps thousands, of non-felons in Florida" were improperly removed from voting rolls. The *Post* also concluded that "it is clear that at least 2,000 felons whose voting rights had been automatically restored in other states were kept off the rolls, and in many cases, denied the right the vote." The *Post* noted that Florida's strict rules against any past felon voting—mirrored and cherished throughout the states of the old Confederacy—resulted in "31 percent of the state's black men" being disqualified as felons.

The Commission documented that the "felon list" supplied by Harris to local election boards had a "14.1-percent error rate." As ConsortiumNews.com notes: "Much of that resulted from overt decisions by Jeb Bush's subordinates to include 'false positives,' that is, people with names, addresses or other data similar to felons."

Florida state official Emmett "Bucky" Mitchell wrote in an e-mail to the Republican contractor who supplied the felon list, "Obviously, we want to capture more names that possibly aren't matches and let the [county election] supervisors make a final determination rather than exclude certain matches altogether." Many county officials claim they weren't given these instructions and that the list was presented to them as known felons without voting rights.

The *Los Angeles Times*, in a May 21 story, reported, "The botched effort to stop felons from voting could have affected the ultimate outcome." The *Times* noted, "The reason: those on the list were disproportionately African-American. Blacks made up 66 percent of those named as felons in Miami-Dade, the state's largest county, for example, and 54 percent in Hillsborough County, which includes Tampa."

Additionally, the *Post* reiterated the obvious: "Black neighborhoods lost more presidential votes than any other areas because of outmoded voting machines and confusion about ballots."

But none dare call it a conspiracy, even though all the data suggest a deliberate and systematic attempt by George W. Bush's brother and his close friend Katherine Harries to disenfranchise black voters.

IMPEACH THE SUPREME COURT'S GANG OF FIVE

Anybody who ever doubted that the 2000 "election" of George W. Bush was in fact a coup d'etat can put those doubts to rest. A trickle of powerful new documents, soon to turn into a tidal wave, irrefutably confirms that this vicious, bumbling airhead stole the presidency. Or rather, it was stolen for him.

Most important is a report from the U.S. Commission on Civil Rights, which got a predictable cold shoulder from the mainstream media. The commission examined the role of racial discrimination in the 2000 vote. There were, as you'll recall, thousands of complaints that African-Americans were turned away from the polls in Florida and other crucial states—especially Tennessee—on dubious pretexts.

Some were stopped in the streets by police and sent home under threat of arrest. Others arrived at polling stations only to be sent to county seats and town halls for absurd non-reasons. In so doing, Florida election officials, under the mandate of Bush's brother Jeb and Secretary of State Katherine Harris (who was also state chair of the Bush campaign), eradicated more than enough potential black/Democratic votes to deny Al Gore the presidency.

Indeed, the Florida Bush administration launched a computerized pre-election attack on black voters by purging alleged felons from voter rolls. Many of those targeted were not felons at all, but merely suspected Democrats—and known African-Americans.

There's no doubt that the number of certain Gore voters purposely driven from the polls by Republicans would have given Gore the presidency. The attack was blatant and conscious. But when the commission's report was issued, the media focused almost entirely on dismissive responses from the Bushes and their cohorts.

Similar media shruggery accompanied a recent study on voting machine error. Among other things, the report revealed a very wide discrepancy between the quality of voting machines in wealthy districts as opposed to poorer ones. Are you surprised to hear that a ballot cast in the inner city—as many as four percent of them—is more than twice as likely to go uncounted as one cast in a suburb?

Seems like a small thing, until you calculate the impact across the U.S. Or in a populous state like Florida. A new study from the Massachusetts and California Institutes of Technology estimates as many as six million votes were discarded by faulty machines in the 2000 election. So this simple "mechanical" discrepancy means that at very least, hundreds of thousands of poorer people's votes are simply pitched in the trash at every election.

Since Al Gore won the 2000 election by more than 500,000 votes that were actually counted, how many more were cast for him that weren't counted? And how many of those would have made the difference in Florida, Tennessee, New Hampshire or West Virginia, any one of which would have kept the Shrub in Texas?

Meanwhile, a top-level investigative team from the *New York Times* has confirmed that while piously trashing legitimate Democratic votes, the Republicans illegally manipulated the overseas ballot count.

According to the *Times*, "The flawed votes included ballots without postmarks, ballots postmarked after the election, ballots without witness signatures, ballots mailed from towns and cities within the United States and even ballots from voters who voted twice. All would have been disqualified had the state's election laws been strictly enforced." But since Bush campaign chair Harris was in control, hundreds of them were counted for Bush while hundreds of contested Gore votes were trashed.

Then there's the U.S. Supreme Court's infamous intervention that stopped the counting of the ballots in key Miami-area counties. The national stench still lingers from that terrible day when the "justices" prevented poll workers from completing a thorough reckoning of how thousands of American citizens wanted to their votes to count.

New books by two prestigious lawyers make it clear that this decision was as cynical, corrupt and illegal as any ever made in U.S. history.

Prosecutor Vincent Bugliosi's *Betrayal of America* correctly says the "Gang of Five" justices who stopped the proper tally of Florida ballots committed treason and should be impeached. Defense Attorney Allen Dershowitz's *Supreme Injustice* methodically dismantles any possible moral, philosophical or legal justification Justices Rehnquist, Scalia, O'Connor, Kennedy or Thomas might have had for throwing the election to George W. Bush.

Briefly: Five right-wing judges—who, throughout their careers, scorned the Constitution's equal protection guarantees when it comes to minorities, the poor and the disadvantaged—somehow contrived to use these same guarantees to "protect" Bush from being harmed by a true accounting of how Floridians actually voted. The theory, if it could be called that, was that if Shrub went to the White House and it was later shown he hadn't won the actual vote count, it would do him "irreparable harm." But Scalia wrote this *before* Bush was actually shown to have won the election!

To make sure Bush did win, five "states' rights" judges trashed a state supreme court whose clear Constitutional duty, established with two centuries of legal precedent, was to guarantee all votes within its jurisdiction were properly counted. The federal court denied Floridians the very counting methods signed into law in Texas by Shrub himself.

The Bush Five made legal history by explicitly limiting their ruling to a single case, again scorning both basic legal logic and 200 years of precedent. And each, individually, contradicted on this case virtually every ruling and every belief established throughout their sorry individual careers over the preceding decades.

There is much more to *Bush v. Gore*. But the unavoidable conclusion of these two impressive volumes is the clear understanding that all the doubt and cynicism that surrounded the Supreme Court's theft of the 2000 election for the Republicans was more than justified. The Gang of Five each had petty personal motives for planting Shrub in the White House in direct conflict with the law of the land and their duties as justices of the Supreme Court.

They guaranteed with this decision that nothing significant about them will matter except their corrupt mediocrity and their venal servicing of the Taliban wing of the Republican Party. They have forever poisoned both the legacy of the Supreme Court and the legitimacy of what's left of the democratic process in this country. When Bugliosi advocates their removal from office, he understates the punishment they deserve.

FITRAKIS

April 18, 2003

DRUGGED OUT AT THE POLLS

The only reason George W. Bush is President today—unleashing the dogs of war and pushing the U.S. into becoming a hard-right, authoritarian and militaristic state—is the unconscionable "war on drugs." Benito Mussolini proved in the 1920s that the tactic works—drug wars are the harbinger of encroaching authoritarianism, as the state utilizes its police forces to disenfranchise voters and silence dissent.

A February 2000 *USA Today* article presciently summed up the impending impact of the drug war on the 2000 election, complete with the usual bar graphic. The key figure, of course, was that 31 percent of Florida's black male population was prevented from voting due to felony convictions. Florida, and 11 other states of the former Confederacy, disenfranchise felons for life, rather than restoring their voting rights after they're released from prison.

During the 2000 election, 13 percent of black men were barred from voting, contrasted to only two percent of white men. The statistics are all too familiar to those who analyze the war on drugs: The federal government tells us that 14 percent of illegal drug users are blacks, but 55 percent of those convicted for drug felonies are black, and 74 percent of all sentenced for drug possession are black.

Why the disparity? There's the usual reasons of racism, fear by the white majority, stereotyping and framing by the media. But a more obvious answer is the politics of the inequality of racial sentencing. The racial and ethnic group most likely to vote Democratic in our society are blacks, with over 90 percent voting for Democratic presidential candidates over the last few decades. George W. Bush could only become President by eliminating as many black voters as possible in key electoral states like Florida.

Moreover, the war on drugs serves another insidious purpose. With the CIA's well-documented ties to drug traffickers as "assets" of U.S. national security, the attack on African-American males not only gives the Bush family power (remember Bush senior was once CIA director) but it keeps the price of drugs high and profitable for friends of the Bush family like Khalid bin Mafusz.

Recall that it was the opium money of the Bank of Credit and Commerce International (BCCI) that funded the former U.S. ally Osama bin Laden and his Al Qaeda network—as well as providing the cash to pay off Dubya when Harken Oil bailed out his failing oil company. It's a classic two-fer: those most likely to vote Democratic are disenfranchised in Florida and Texas, and the CIA's allies reap record profit because the phony drug war makes the plentiful and naturally grown narcotics artificially valuable. Two fer the price of one.

Essentially, the drug war and felony disenfranchisement served the same purpose in the 2000 election as the old Jim Crow-era poll tax, a tax on voting that made it difficult for blacks to participate.

As U.S. Representative John Conyers Jr. pointed out, "If we want former felons to become good citizens, we must give them rights as well as responsibilities, and there is no greater responsibility than voting."

Judge Albie Sachs of South Africa's Constitutional Court echoes this theme: "The vote of each and every citizen is a badge of dignity and personhood. Quite literally, everyone counts."

Unfortunately, because the Bush family has learned to count electoral votes, not every citizen counts in the United States. This, of course, makes their right-wing allies on the Supreme Court, like Chief Justice William Rehnquist, apologists for the denial of voting rights. As Rehnquist has commented, "The majority determines the rights of the minority"—a train of thought that runs contrary to that of the Constitution's architect, James Madison.

The 15th Amendment to the U.S. Constitution stated, "The rights of citizens of the United States to vote shall not be denied or abridged by the United States or by any State on account of race, color or previous condition of servitude." Although not enforced by the U.S. until the passage of the Voting Rights Act of 1965, the actual year the U.S. became a minimal democracy, the law mandates that one cannot be denied the right to vote "on account of race or color."

Nevertheless, by instituting a systematically racist war on drugs, the far right of the Republican Party can claim that they are acting fairly and impartially by imprisoning drug felons rather than black males. This is much like the old "grandfather" clause, struck down in 1915 by the U.S. Supreme Court, which allowed everyone in a former Confederate state to vote after Reconstruction, provided their grandfathers had voted in that state.

As if the unconscionable drug war wasn't enough to fuel their Florida coup, the Bush boys further disenfranchised tens of thousands of black voters who had the misfortunate of having names that were "the same or similar" to the names of felons. The computerized purge of voting rolls engineered by Dubya's brother Jeb and Florida's Secretary of State Katherine Harris deliberately targeted all "John Smiths" (or Jon Smiths or John Smithes) if one John Smith happened to have been busted for smoking a joint. Talk about guilt by association—or rather, complete lack of association. Ironically, many U.S. blacks have similar names because the slavery system required them to take the names of their slave owners.

Also ironic is that Dubya's admitted two decades of substance abuse and the allegations of cocaine use, which he refuses to deny, would have most likely made him ineligible to be President or even to vote in Florida, had he been convicted of a drug felony. Lucky for Bush he's not black—that drug war can be hell.

PART TWO

AMERICA'S REICHSTAG FIRES?

CALL IT OPERATION BLOWBACK

Threa CIA's famous word for unintended consequences—"blowback"—explains it all: bin Laden, Al Qaeda, the Taliban. It's a good thing Americans are notoriously ahistorical. Otherwise they might remember how the U.S. installed Pakistani military dictator General Zia ul-Haq in 1977. They might also remember President Jimmy Carter's National Security Advisor, Zbigniew Brzezinski—wearing a bizarre turban that looked like it was borrowed from an Indian Sikh rather than an Afghan warrior—standing on the border of the Soviet Union and shouting to the Mujaheddin to "wage a jihad!" against the Communists. In the summer of 1979, Brzezinski advised Carter to sign a secret directive to support the fledgling Mujaheddin movement. That was six months before Soviet tanks rolled into Kabul.

In a series of articles and books, Brzezinski, a former Columbia University professor, analyzed how the multi-ethnic Soviet Union could be destroyed through inflaming the religious passions of 50 million to 60 million Central Asian Muslims.

The Mujaheddin took the message to heart. They're now waging a jihad against us.

Soon after the anti-Soviet jihad began, Dan Rather, in more authentic headgear, broadcast live alongside what he called "Afghan freedom fighters...who were engaged in a deeply patriotic fight to the death for home and hearth."

Rather made heroes of Afghan opium runners like Yunas Khalis, who fought to control Afghanistan's poppy fields more than he fought the Soviets. Seven heroin labs near Khalis' headquarters in Ribat helped fund the jihad. U.S. taxpayers kicked in too, through the construction of an irrigation system in the Helmand Valley, where 60 percent of Afghanistan's opium grows.

The Reagan administration enthusiastically joined the jihad against the Soviets. The concomitant drugs and arms bazaar flourished in the northwest Pakistan town of Darra with America's loyal allies, the Pakistani Inter-Service Intelligence, regulating both the opium and arms trades to the Mujaheddin.

The U.S. government pressured China, Egypt and Saudi Arabia to support the covert operation. Egyptian President Anwar Sadat remarked shortly before his assassination by the Mujaheddin network that "The U.S. contacted me, they told me, 'Please open your stores for us so that we can give the Afghans the arms they need to fight.'" Sadat was the first famous casualty of the blowback.

The Saudi royal family, despite pressure, declined direct participation. Instead they sent Osama bin Laden—the son of one of Saudi Arabia's wealthiest citizens—to Afghanistan. Government records indicate the CIA's covert action in creating the Mujaheddin and bin Laden's terrorist apparatus cost $3.2 billion, the most expensive covert operation in the CIA's history.

So lucrative was the opium and drug business in the Golden Crescent—where Afghanistan, Pakistan and Iran meet—the off-shore accounts in Pakistan's largest bank, Habib, overflowed. The Bank of Credit and Commerce International (BCCI), founded by Agha Hasan Abedi, pitched in to help with the money laundering and became notorious as the most corrupt bank in world history. BCCI now stands for the Bank of Crooks and Criminals International, after going belly-up in 1991 with a reported $20 billion missing.

Well there's bound to be some wealth generated when, according to DEA documents, 40 heroin syndicates were operating in Pakistan in the mid-1980s through an estimated 200 heroin manufacturing facilities.

In May 1984, Vice President George Bush traveled to Pakistan to confer with our dictator, General Zia. Bush the Elder, the former CIA director, handed the drug problem over to the CIA, despite its notorious history of involvement with cocaine traffickers in Central America and heroin trafficking in Central Asia. Bush granted the CIA primary responsibility for controlling drug informants and other "assets" in the Golden Crescent.

By 1989, the Soviets were in full retreat from Afghanistan while bin Laden and his Mujaheddin and Taliban allies were firmly in control of heroin traffic in Central Asia. Bin Laden's biographer, Yossef Bodansky, envisioned BCCI as a "world bank for fundamentalists" before its collapse.

In 1992, the U.S. Senate's Foreign Relations Committee issued a massive report on the BCCI scandal. If you want to understand where bin Laden's money came from—though the media originally reported he inherited $300 million from his father, they've now correctly adjusted that to $20 million—you need to know of BCCI's role in the world of guns and drugs. You might want to start with Section 13 of the Senate report, titled "BCCI, the CIA and Foreign Intelligence."

Caught up in the scandal were Jimmy Carter's ethically challenged former Director of the Office of Management and Budget, Bert Lance, former Secretary of Defense Clark Clifford and other infamous individuals. The Senate's BCCI report recommended further investigation was needed into "international criminal financier Mark Rich."

Remember Rich—the guy pardoned by Bill Clinton? The report states, "Rich's commodities firms were used by BCCI in connection with BCCI's involve[ment] in U.S. guaranteed programs through the Department of Agriculture."

BCCI funds also allegedly financed the controversial WTI incinerator in eastern Ohio with the Swiss firm Von Roll. Four of Von Roll's top officials were convicted for selling material for the Iraqi "Supergun." Government documents also link WTI to Mafia families in the U.S. and the incinerator was involved in a political money-laundering scandal connected to Ohio Governor George Voinovich's administration.

The *Times of London* reported shortly after the September 11 attacks that Deloitte and Touche, the accounting firm, was being dragged into the hunt for Osama bin Laden's terror network. The *Times* reported that BCCI was used to launder terrorist money and as the chief depository for

CIA covert funds paid to bin Laden during the Afghan war with the Soviets.

The *St. Louis Post-Dispatch* also noted, "Before it [BCCI] was shut down in 1991, it was used to fund the Mujaheddin, then fighting the Soviet-supported government of Afghanistan. The money came from U.S. and Saudi intelligence."

It's blowback time indeed.

WASSERMAN
November 1, 2001

AMERICA'S TERRORIST NUCLEAR THREAT TO ITSELF

N o sane nation hands to a wartime enemy atomic weapons set to go off within its own homeland, and then lights the fuse. Yet as the bombs and missiles drop on Afghanistan, the certainty of terror retaliation inside America has turned our 103 nuclear power plants into weapons of apocalyptic destruction, just waiting to be used against us.

One or both of the planes that crashed into the World Trade Center on September 11 could have easily obliterated the two atomic reactors now operating at Indian Point, New York, about 40 miles up the Hudson.

The catastrophic devastation would have been unfathomable. But those and a hundred other American reactors are still running. Security has been heightened. But all are vulnerable to another sophisticated terror attack aimed at perpetrating the unthinkable.

Indian Point Unit One was shut long ago by public outcry. But Units Two and Three have operated since the 1970s. Back then there was talk of requiring reactor containment domes to be strong enough to withstand a jetliner crash. But the biggest jets were far smaller than the ones that fly today. Nor did those early calculations account for the onboard jet fuel, whose hellish fire melted the critical steel supports that ultimately brought down the Twin Towers.

Had one or both those jets hit one or both the operating reactors at Indian Point, the ensuing cloud of radiation would have dwarfed the ones at Hiroshima and Nagasaki, Three Mile Island and Chernobyl.

The intense radioactive heat within today's operating reactors is the hottest anywhere on the planet. So are the hellish levels of radioactivity.

Because Indian Point has operated so long, its accumulated radioactive burden far exceeds that of Chernobyl, which ran only four years before it exploded.

Some believe the World Trade Center jets could have collapsed or breached either of the Indian Point containment domes. But at very least the massive impact and intense jet fuel fire would destroy the human ability to control the plants' functions. Vital cooling systems, backup power generators and communications networks would crumble.

Indeed, Indian Point Unit One was shut because activists warned that its lack of an emergency core cooling system made it an unacceptable risk. The government ultimately agreed.

But today terrorist attacks could destroy those same critical cooling and control systems that are vital to not only the Unit Two and Three reactor cores, but to the spent fuel pools that sit on site.

The assault would not require a large jet. The safety systems are extremely complex and virtually indefensible. One or more could be wiped out with a wide range of easily deployed small aircraft, ground-based weapons, truck bombs or even chemical/biological assaults aimed at the operating work force. Dozens of U.S. reactors have repeatedly failed even modest security tests over the years. Even heightened wartime standards cannot guarantee protection of the vast, supremely sensitive controls required for reactor safety.

Without continuous monitoring and guaranteed water flow, the thousands of tons of radioactive rods in the cores and the thousands more stored in those fragile pools would rapidly melt into super-hot radioactive balls of lava that would burn into the ground and the water table and, ultimately, the Hudson.

Indeed, a jet crash like the one on September 11 or other forms of terrorist assault at Indian Point could yield three infernal fireballs of molten radioactive lava burning through the earth and into the aquifer and the river. Striking water they would blast gigantic billows of horribly radioactive steam into the atmosphere. Prevailing winds from the north and west might initially drive these clouds of mass death downriver into New York City and east into Westchester and Long Island.

But at Three Mile Island and Chernobyl, winds ultimately shifted around the compass to irradiate all surrounding areas with the devastating poisons released by the on-going fiery torrent. At Indian Point, thousands of square miles would have been saturated with the most lethal clouds ever created or imagined, depositing relentless genetic poisons that would kill forever.

In nearby communities like Buchanan, Nyack, Monsey and scores more, infants and small children would quickly die en masse. Virtually all pregnant women would spontaneously abort, or ultimately give birth to horribly deformed offspring. Ghastly sores, rashes, ulcerations and burns would afflict the skin of millions. Emphysema, heart attacks, stroke, multiple organ failure, hair loss, nausea, inability to eat or drink or swallow, diarrhea and incontinence, sterility and impotence, asthma, blindness and more would kill thousands on the spot, and doom hundreds of thousands if not millions.

A terrible metallic taste would afflict virtually everyone downwind in New York, New Jersey and New England, a ghoulish curse similar to that endured by the fliers who dropped the atomic bombs on Hiroshima and Nagaskai, by those living downwind from nuclear bomb tests in the South Seas and Nevada, and by victims caught in the downdrafts from Three Mile Island and Chernobyl.

Then comes the abominable wave of cancers, leukemias, lymphomas, tumors and hellish diseases for which new names will have to be invented, and new dimensions of agony will beg description.

Indeed, those who survived the initial wave of radiation would envy those who did not.

Evacuation would be impossible, but thousands would die trying. Bridges and highways would become killing fields for those attempting to escape to destinations that would soon enough become equally deadly as the winds shifted.

Attempts to quench the fires would be futile. At Chernobyl, pilots flying helicopters that dropped boron on the fiery core died in droves. At Indian Point, such missions would be a sure ticket to death. Their utility would be doubtful anyway, as the molten cores rage uncontrolled for days, weeks and years, spewing ever more devastation into the eco-sphere. More than 800,000 Soviet draftees were forced through Chernobyl's seething remains in a futile attempt to clean it up. They are dying in droves. Who would now volunteer for such an American task force?

The radioactive cloud from Chernobyl blanketed the vast Ukraine and Belarus landscape, then carried over Europe and into the jetstream, surging through the West Coast of the United States within 10 days, carrying across our northern tier, circling the globe, then coming back again.

The radioactive clouds from Indian Point would enshroud New York, New Jersey, New England and carry deep into the Atlantic and up into Canada and across to Europe and around the globe again and again.

The immediate damage would render thousands of the world's most populous and expensive square miles permanently uninhabitable. All five boroughs of New York City would be an apocalyptic wasteland. The World Trade Center would be rendered as unusable and even more lethal by a jet crash at Indian Point than it was by the direct hits of September 11. All real estate and economic value would be poisonously radioactive through-out the entire region. Irreplaceable trillions in human capital would be for-ever lost.

As at Three Mile Island, where thousands of farm and wild animals died in heaps, and as at Chernobyl, where soil, water and plant life have been hopelessly irradiated, natural ecosystems on which human and all other life depend would be permanently and irrevocably destroyed.

Spiritually, psychologically, financially, ecologically—our nation would never recover. This is what we missed by a mere 40 miles near New York City on September 11.

There are 103 of these potential Bombs of the Apocalypse now operat-ing in the United States. They generate just 18 percent of America's elec-tricity, just eight percent of our total energy. As with reactors elsewhere, the two at Indian Point have both been off-line for long periods of time with no appreciable impact on life in New York. Already an extremely expensive source of electricity, the cost of attempting to defend these reactors will put nuclear energy even further off the competitive scale.

Since its deregulation crisis, California—already the nation's second-most efficient state—cut further into its electric consumption by some 15 percent. Within a year the U.S. could cheaply replace with increased effi-ciency all the reactors now so much more expensive to operate and protect.

Yet, as the bombs fall and the terror escalates, Congress is fast-tracking a form of legal immunity to protect the operators of reactors like Indian Point from liability in case of a meltdown or terrorist attack.

Why is our nation handing its proclaimed enemies the weapons of our own mass destruction, and then shielding from liability the companies that insist on continuing to operate them?

Do we take this war seriously? Are we committed to the survival of our nation?

If so, the ticking reactor bombs that could obliterate the very core of our life and of all future generations must be shut down.

THE WAR PROFITEERS

The hottest circles of Hell are reserved for those who profit from the misfortunes of others. None is worse than those who profit from war. As our bombers pummel Afghanistan, and as our Constitutional rights are shredded in the name of patriotism, the corporate hogs are snorting at the public trough.

Under cover of national emergency, waving their flags, they are greedily gouging us in ways not possible under peacetime scrutiny. Indeed, soon after the September 11 bombing, the *Wall Street Journal* published an infamous piece urging conservatives and corporations to cash in on Bush's windfall popularity.

Here are a few of the most grotesque profiteers:

The Nuke Pushers: After 30 years of heated debate, the reality that terrorists could blow up an atomic reactor and inflict incalculable damage seems to have finally sunk in among the media, the public and even some members of government. The Nuclear Regulatory Commission now admits U.S. reactors cannot withstand a jet crash. The National Guard has been dispatched to many of America's 103 reactors and flight paths have been altered. But the obvious step—shutting them all down—has not been discussed. Also unmentioned: Who will pay for all this heightened security?

When all real costs are tallied, nukes are our most expensive form of energy, even without the added security costs. Reactors provide just 18 percent of our electricity, just eight percent of our energy—easily replaceable with cheaper, safer, cleaner and more reliable efficiency and conservation, not to mention renewable wind and solar power. But the nuke pushers own the Bush administration and Congress. So while we pay to keep the reactors running under siege, the industry demands renewal of the 1957 Price-Anderson Act, shielding it from any liability in case of an accident or sabotage. Next time a nuke flack lies about reactor safety, ask: "Why can't you get your own private insurance?"

The Star Warriors: September 11 proved the utter worthlessness of an anti-missile defense system. But the big weapons merchants still want a whole new level of militarism in outer space, which is what this "missile shield" nonsense is really all about. Cashing in on the inevitable flag waving, the rocketeers took another $8 billion in pure pork.

The Oil Barons: The petroleum partners in the White House and Congress are sleazing through this national tragedy with an energy plan larded with hype. For example, drilling the Alaska National Wildlife Refuge is allegedly to help us get off foreign oil. But since the first embargo in 1973, the oil barons have squashed the promise of an alternative energy economy based on renewable sources and efficiency. So we now import more oil than ever.

The latest patriotic gimmick is pumping still more oil through an 800-mile above-ground pipeline, which a drunken hunter recently mistook for a giant polar anaconda. His single bullet shut down the entire line while creating a major environmental disaster. So what could an actual terrorist do to this multi-billion-dollar, ecologically suicidal "lifeline"? How about this time we go solar?

The Usual Corporate Suspects: Under cover of war, the administration is pushing a gargantuan "stimulus package" that's little more than a huge tax rebate—dating back to the mid-1990s—for the greediest and seediest of our corporate giants. Up there is Enron, the Houston gas giant that's poured millions into Republican coffers. Led by Bush crony Kenneth Lay, Enron seemed a rare corporate success story until a recent torrent of news about mismanagement and possible illegalities poured into the Internet. Enron tried to leap from fossil fuels to electronic data transmission but melted down. So now the "free market" Republicans want to reward their failure with our money.

The Airlines: Nobody has failed America more dramatically than the airlines. In the spirit of deregulation they've refused for years to meet basic security standards. Much of the blame for September 11 lies with their greed-driven refusal to put locks on cockpit doors, place marshals on flights and actually pay security personnel. As "retribution" for their disgraceful sloth, they got more than $15 billion of our money, laid off thousands of innocent workers and took huge executive bonuses.

The Eco-Destroyers: Under cover of war, Gail Norton's Interior Department is shredding whatever environmental protections we had left, slipping huge public giveaways to the mining, timber and cattle industries, among the many. Meanwhile, watch the Homeland Security Force use its anti-terror powers to attack the non-violent environmental movement. As Joe McCarthy would say, it'll be déjà vu all over again.

The Drug Warriors: Lost in the World Trade Center dust were the millions of anti-opium dollars Bush poured into Taliban coffers as recently as this past spring. Osama bin Laden and his Afghan fascists are as much a product of the drug war as of oil. Throughout the Third World, the official approach to our national drug problem has been akin to an overweight man attempting to cure his overeating by blowing up certain bakeries and killing people who make flour. Since the 1970s the U.S. has spent countless billions poisoning plants and imprisoning pot smokers. If that money had been used to actually protect us from terrorism, the World Trade Towers might still be standing.

December 27, 2001

THE TYRANT'S SNEER

America is no longer America. The civil liberties and basic freedoms of speech, press, assembly, privacy and private property on which this country was founded have been decimated by the Bush regime, and worse is likely to come.

Long before September 11 the administration established its bent for autocratic secrecy and intolerance. Now Attorney General John Ashcroft, long an enemy of the First Amendment, is using the tragedies in ways akin to the cynical dictatorships the U.S. has put in power throughout the Third World. Piling the war against terrorism onto the war on drugs, the administration is staging an unprecedented assault against our basic rights.

For decades, the harsh, arbitrary and overwhelmingly racist nature of the drug war has given police free reign to slash away at our civil rights and liberties. It has encouraged, among other things, the arbitrary seizure of private property without even a court hearing. Americans are allowed—encouraged—to consume alcohol and tobacco, but imprisoned for consuming a wide range of other substances that are far safer.

Since being declared by Richard Nixon in the 1970s, this war on the general public has consumed hundreds of billions of dollars in policing, prison expenses and social devastation. Several hundred thousand

Americans now sit in local, state and federal prisons for drug-related offenses. By a vast margin, those jailed are disproportionately people of color, among other things denying them their right to vote. Disenfranchised black prisoners in Florida alone could have put Al Gore in the White House.

Last spring George W. Bush gave Afghanistan's Taliban regime some $38 million, ostensibly to fight opium production. Millions continue to flow to allegedly anti-drug death squads throughout Latin America and elsewhere. Meanwhile, GOP "states' rights conservatives" use federal powers (as did the Clinton administration) to trash eight state referenda where voters solidly approved the right to use medical marijuana.

Bush now says he'll prosecute health food stores that sell products containing hemp oil, used for centuries as a medicinal and nutritional ingredient. He may also ban clothing and other fabrics made with hemp fiber, used since Biblical times for countless products, including the paper on which the Declaration of Independence was written.

Also before September 11, Bush, by executive order, barred public access to a wide range of presidential papers dating back decades. This unprecedented anti-democratic edict has horrified mainstream scholars and even staunch conservatives.

Meanwhile, Vice President Dick Cheney has defied congressional requests that he identify the corporate chieftains with whom he secretly concocted the administration's energy plan. This anti-green grab bag of huge oil, coal and nuclear subsidies apparently was drafted primarily by Kenneth Lay, Bush's close personal friend and largest donor. Lay just led his Houston-based Enron Corporation into the biggest bankruptcy in U.S. history, while himself walking away with at least $100 million in personal compensation.

As the first modern President to take the White House without a national majority, Bush was well on his way to being its most repressive when September 11 hit. The crashes have perfectly served the administration's ongoing assault on the Bill of Rights. Among other things, the White House has:

• Established military tribunals empowered to use secret proceedings to execute suspects denied the right to mount a defense or even see the evidence against them. Right-wing columnist William Safire branded the tribunals a step toward "dictatorial power" and a "dismaying departure from due process."

• Announced it would monitor conversations between prisoners and their attorneys, a clear violation of the Bill of Rights.

• Detained more than a thousand people without public notification or trial or access to attorneys or loved ones, bringing to the U.S. the classic fascist technique of "disappearing" suspected opponents.

• Asked to use secret evidence to prosecute deportations without providing that evidence to the defense.

• Vastly expanded federal powers of wiretapping, Internet monitoring, search and seizure, warrant-less detention and denial of the rights of speech and assembly.

• Laid the groundwork for a national identity card.

• Moved toward the universal use of facial screening, a bizarre technique where video cameras in public places are used to identify "suspicious" or "criminal-looking" citizens.

• And warned the press and public to curb criticism of the Bush regime, or face reprisals.

The administration's defining motto is now "watch what you say," uttered by menacing press secretary Ari Fleischer in a now-classic moment broadcast over national airwaves. Equating dissent with terrorism is the official order of the day. Newspaper and TV commentators who dare criticize the administration have lost their jobs.

Ashcroft threatened Congress with a sneering attack on its right to question his shredding of the Bill of Rights. Ashcroft has a long history of contempt for civil rights and liberties, a dictatorial and racist streak angrily vetted in his bitter confirmation hearings. Since September 11 the Attorney General has reveled in payback time, explicitly impugning the patriotism and loyalty of anyone daring to oppose him.

Police throughout the country have followed suit with increasingly aggressive assaults on nonviolent demonstrations for peace. The FBI has been given the green light to infiltrate and disrupt citizen organizations, reviving the infamous COINTELPRO operations J. Edgar Hoover used to destroy peace and civil rights groups throughout the 1960s and 1970s and to attack Martin Luther King.

The administration has shamelessly wrapped the horrors of September 11 around massive subsidies for the corporations that put it in power. Most recently it has implied that a vote against "fast-track" trade handouts was a vote for terrorism. A cowed U.S. House approved new autocratic powers for Bush by one vote.

A wide range of Constitutional scholars and even hardcore conservatives now warn that this is the most ruthless attack on our basic rights in all of U.S. history. It's being done in the name of a war on terrorism; but, as the great Molly Ivins has put it: "We can make ourselves less free, and all we'll be is less free, not safer."

With a compliant media and a docile Congress, it's not foreign terrorists that most seriously threaten our cherished freedoms. It's the White House.

WASSERMAN

January 17, 2002

THE AMERICAN DICTATOR

The American people are in deep denial. The football playoffs have bulled ahead. The soaps are on the air. The economy is down but not crashed. And the nation is on the brink of dictatorship, stumbling after the tragedy of September 11 toward another disastrous 30-year drug-style war against our rights and freedoms. Whether we come out of it with anything resembling a real democracy remains to be seen.

All Americans should understand that the basic liberties won in our great national revolution 225 years ago have been obliterated in the last 90 days. Our most sacred document, the Bill of Rights, has been shredded. Arbitrary arrest, imprisonment and even execution are now at the unchecked whim of the federal executive. Powers only dreamed of by Britain's imperial King George III are now at the fingertips of George Bush II.

Bush's demeanor is amiable and reassuring. But the powers he and his Attorney General, John Ashcroft, have seized for themselves and those who will follow are profoundly more threatening than any ever taken by a U.S. executive.

On paper, the United States after September 11, 2001, now resembles the brutal dictatorship of Chile after the U.S.-sponsored coup of September 11, 1973, when the CIA and Henry Kissinger helped the vicious thug

Augusto Pinochet destroy a democratically elected government. In the ensuing years, thousands of private citizens disappeared, never to be seen again. Freedom of speech, press, assembly and other human basic rights were obliterated.

In Chile, it was all in the name of fighting communism; here, the official line is "if it helps fight terrorism, it must be OK."

But the Bush/Ashcroft commitment to the real safety of the American public is far less firm than its commitment to certain key supporters, like the National Rifle Association and Enron.

Such contradictions are currently buried under Bush's much-trumpeted 90-percent approval ratings. But what do such ratings mean amidst White House threats to "watch what you say"? Even slightly critical media commentators now lose their jobs or air time. Case in point: Bill Maher, whose *Politically Incorrect* was canned by local TV stations nationwide for a single off-handed and misquoted remark which was in the long-standing spirit of his show.

The American major media is now owned by six corporations, all with very substantial financial interests wrapped up in the Bush administration. None has the courage to criticize it. None allows equal time to alternative voices. Nor has there been a peep as the administration uses executive orders to block public access to basic government data, and to lock up all presidential papers since 1980, thus protecting, among others, the President's father.

In that spirit, Attorney General Ashcroft has also assaulted the First Amendment's guarantees of free speech and assembly and Fourth Amendment protections against unwarranted search and seizure. But he grovels to the National Rifle Association's view of the Second Amendment's umbrella over gun ownership. Incredibly, the administration has warned citizens to "watch what you say," but in an undeclared war against errant violence, refuses to track gun owners. Since September 11 it's become far more dangerous to speak your mind, but it's as easy as ever to buy and hide a gun.

Likewise, in service to its backers from the airline industry, but to the detriment of public safety, the administration has resisted basic (but expensive) improvements in flight security. It has refused to disclose the full extent of bankrupt Enron's participation in drafting a pro-oil, pro-gas, anti-efficiency national energy plan and, incredibly, denies even talking to

Bush's close personal friend Kenneth "Kenny-Boy" Lay as the company headed to disaster.

Bush has also refused to defuse the nation's 103 commercial atomic power plants. These ticking nuclear time bombs are potential terrorist targets with unimaginable potential fallout. An administration that has taken millions from the corporations that own them has inexcusably left the American public vulnerable to their horrors.

The administration has also done nothing to wean the nation off the root cause of this crisis, oil. Raising the average fuel efficiency of our national auto fleet to 40 miles per gallon would allow the U.S. to stop importing oil altogether. But in service to the auto and oil industries, the administration is fighting those standards, pushing instead for increased drilling in places like Alaska, where pipelines are sitting ducks for even amateur terrorists.

Meanwhile, Bush and Ashcroft continue to spew time, money and effort on a partisan right-wing agenda that has nothing to do with public safety. Atop the list is the 30-year war on drugs, which may be the tragic model for the "war on terrorism."

Thanks largely to the hugely expensive drug war fiasco, the U.S. now has a larger percentage of its population behind bars than any other nation on earth, surpassing both Russia and China. More than six million Americans are either in jail, on probation or otherwise charged. Hundreds of thousands of these cases involve marijuana, which seven states have now declared a valued medicinal substance.

The American gulag features a terrible arsenal of barbaric punishments, including widespread rape. Its prime political use is to detain dissidents and people of color and rob them of the right to vote.

Tens of millions of Americans regularly smoke marijuana and see nothing wrong with it. New research confirms its value in fighting rheumatoid arthritis along with its well-established uses in cases of cancer, AIDS, glaucoma and other diseases.

In prosecuting the use of such a popular substance, the government has arrogated the power to imprison virtually anyone, according to its whim, with absolutely no impact on marijuana use and no end in sight.

Anti-terror will now expand the gulag indefinitely. Like the war on drugs, the terror war has an ephemeral enemy. Bush and Ashcroft want another war without end against an enemy that can never be defined or beaten. Their focus has nothing to do with fighting terrorism, everything to do with enhancing their own power and serving their corporate sponsors.

Those Americans who believe they will be unaffected are dreaming. Under the anti-terror laws, as with the anti-drug laws, virtually everyone is subject to arbitrary arrest and imprisonment.

Ultimately, the war against terrorism will prove just as futile, and just as destructive of our democracy as the war on drugs. America will be less safe, not more. And you will pay yet again with your money, your rights, your freedom.

WASSERMAN

February 21, 2002

ENRON ICEBERG DEAD AHEAD

The Enron Iceberg has struck America's economic *Titanic*, now sinking fast at the incompetent hands of a corrupt President and his criminal cabinet. Needless to say, the Shrub elite is already crammed into the only lifeboat, beating back the masses from steerage with autocratic attacks on the civil liberties and basic freedoms that once made this country great.

Let's tally the losses.

For starters, Enron sabotaged much of what was once the world's biggest and most reliable electric power industry. By buying (or renting) two dozen state legislatures, starting with California, the Houston-based methane pusher wrecked the century-old production and delivery system that powered U.S. prosperity.

California's deregulation disaster fed a $100 billion looting. Illinois, Michigan, Ohio, Pennsylvania and Texas are among the major industrial states whose core power systems are also being pillaged. Enron's self-serving tripe about the wonders of fictional competition in electricity could ultimately cost the nation a cool trillion bucks or more.

So will its cancerous financial corruption. As our seventh-largest corporation, Enron's fiscal criminality reached levels unseen in U.S. history. Its poisonous heap of hidden partnerships festered in the Bush-run safe haven of Texas. Now Bush is cynically blocking the rigorous reforms needed to restore public trust, crippling the long-term credibility of American business as a whole.

Indeed, an administration packed with Enron executives, investors and apologists will hide from the truth for as long as the courts that put them in power will allow. Bush's denials of his close personal friendship with Enron founder Kenneth Lay are loathsome and ludicrous. So are Vice President Dick Cheney's attempts to hide the fact that Enron wrote the Bush Energy Plan. There's enough Enron-related corruption in the executive branch and its regulatory agencies to keep a dozen special prosecutors employed for years. But it's a tribute to Enron's power that countless taxpayer millions were spent on special prosecutors to investigate Bill Clinton's sorry sex life, but so far there's no parallel probe into the illegal dealings of "Kenny-Boy" and his minions.

Likewise the gargantuan pork fest that is the Bush military budget. Since September 11, all eyes have been on Afghanistan, where the U.S. pummeled an unpopular bunch of psychopaths, the Taliban, to which Bush gave $38 million last spring. The trashing of this hapless junta hid the failure to find Osama bin Laden. Drunk with temporarily high poll ratings, Bush is indulging in a $400 billion orgy of military spending perfectly designed to protect Europe from an invasion by the Soviet Union.

Not one of the star wars and heavy metal megabucks being squandered on U.S. defense contractors will do squat to protect U.S. citizens from terrorism. But the cash gushing out of taxpayer pockets into Cold War-style projects will devastate our long-term economic health. Add still more gargantuan expenditures for the repressive, useless and massively expensive drug war, then throw in Bush tax cuts moving billions from working people to the super-rich, and we're looking at the time-honored Republican recipe for economic catastrophe.

This has been sold to Congress and the public with Enron-style budget numbers. To spend, spend and spend still more on regressive and ecologically catastrophic programs that do nothing to serve public needs guarantees the nation a short ride off a steep fiscal cliff.

All this comes courtesy of the cynical exploitation of September 11, a right-wing feeding frenzy originally facilitated by the refusal of deregulated airlines to pay for proper security. The administration is still fighting even that, along with equally obvious preventative measures like shutting down nuclear plants and taking the nation off its dependency on oil and its absurdly vulnerable pipelines.

Indeed, while industrial Europe—especially Germany—races toward true energy independence, George W. Bush's America plunges ever-deeper into its suicidal addiction to nuclear and fossil fuels. Germany, Sweden and Italy have all moved to shut their nuclear reactors while rapidly converting to wind, solar and energy efficiency. Even France, the atom's poster child, has stopped building nuclear reactors and is buying into wind power.

But Bush is still owned by the fossil-fuel and nuclear-power dinosaurs epitomized by Enron. Now he's approved the massively flawed nuke dump scheduled for Yucca Mountain, Nevada. And he's announced the ultimate terrorist act—building a new breed of nuclear reactors. Meanwhile the administration fights against higher fuel efficiency for automobiles, opposes mass transit and refuses to fund a solar industry which is about to hit critical mass.

All of which may be hiding Enron's larger role in a technological revolution. Many energy experts have long said natural gas would be the bridging fuel from a fossil-based system to one fueled by the sun, wind and hydrogen. Enron's 1990s push for deregulation seemed an expression of gas' new position; now Enron's failure may signal that natural gas is due to fade. Its price has soared, it's easily monopolized and it's a serious greenhouse gas.

By contrast, wind power is now the cheapest, most reliable source of new electric production. Photovoltaic cells (which transform sunlight directly into electricity) are close behind. Mass-produced fuel cells are no more than five years away.

In other words, the solar revolution is underway. Whether Enron's crash stands for a weakening of the role of natural gas or the mere escalation of corporate greed on an unprecedented scale remains to be seen.

But clearly Enron is the ultimate monument to a thoroughly corrupt and cynical junta hell-bent on repeating all of Herbert Hoover's worst mistakes. Small wonder the Bushies are also assaulting the basic civil rights and liberties that once made this country great.

Governmental repression is always a sure sign of corruption at the top. The Bushies are right to fear an angry mass opposition, armed with the truth. It's the one thing that can stop this Enronista horde from turning their corporate collapse into a truly global catastrophe.

ATOMIC TERROR ALERT

So if Bush knew something at some time about the possibility of terrorists using jets to crash into government buildings, why didn't he do something about it before September 11? And far more important: If he knows something about the possibility of terrorists attacking atomic power plants and causing a radioactive apocalypse, why doesn't he act *right now*, before we find ourselves in post-tragedy hearings about why he didn't?

And just for the heck of it, let's ask another related question: What do you do with a gigantic, highly radioactive piece of metal that weighs 120 tons, has a six-inch hole in its head and is currently "ship-in-a-bottle" locked inside a massive concrete and steel containment dome that's many feet thick, latticed with powerful rebar steel, allegedly designed to withstand the radioactive fires and pressures of a controlled nuclear explosion?

The rap that U.S. intelligence should have anticipated the possibility of a horrific hijacking like September 11 is not a partisan bauble. The threats were always credible, and there was a way to deal with them—pay for decent airport security.

Paul Krugman of the *New York Times* placed the blame precisely where it belonged immediately after the disaster: airline deregulation. Terrorists don't walk onto commercial aircraft with box cutters unless screening is really lax, which it certainly was prior to September 11. Why? Because the airline industry, with its well-heeled lobbyists working Congress and the White House, didn't want to pay for real precautions. Locks on cockpit doors, armed marshals riding shotgun, trained screening personnel—it wasn't really rocket science. It could have prevented September 11.

But the White House, Senate Majority Leader Tom Daschle (whose wife lobbies for the airlines) and an army of bought politicians simply said: "Don't bother."

Well, now there are prices to be paid. Bush's poll ratings won't shield him from having exploited a horrible human tragedy for which his own corrupt neglect was partly responsible.

But there's another nightmare in the wings, and the response has been as lax and complacent as what led to September 11. But this time the consequences could be infinitely worse.

The major media is now carrying reports of terrorist threats against commercial atomic power plants to happen on or around July 4. Nuke sabotage has long been considered a credible threat. Bush cited reactor plans found at Al Qaeda hideouts and the Ayotallah Khomeini among others has talked about hitting "nuclear targets."

In short, if warnings of hijacked planes crashing into government buildings prior to September 11 were vague and isolated, warnings of attacks on nuclear plants are clear and abundant.

So has the government reacted? Not hardly. There's been some heightened ground security and talk of posting snipers. The Nuclear Control Institute has suggested installing anti-aircraft emplacements. But atomic reactors are infinitely complex and vulnerable. There are literally thousands of ways to attack one. The only real security measure is to shut them all down.

Which is doable. The U.S. electric grid is awash in capacity. The alleged "shortages" driving prices through the California roof were fake. Every reactor in the country could disappear tomorrow and there might be some temporary shortages in some isolated areas, but virtually no impact on the national supply.

Where there *would* be an impact is if one of these threats comes true, a la September 11. A U.S. reactor catastrophe, terrorist or otherwise, could kill hundreds of thousands of people, poison millions, cause trillions of dollars in damage, permanently devastate thousands of square miles and irrevocably cripple the entire U.S. economy. The threats to make all that happen are far clearer and more tangible than what preceded September 11. The administration's insane response has been to push to build more reactors.

So do we wait for disaster to strike and then hold hearings to determine what the administration knew and when? Or do we find a way to shut these things down before the unthinkable occurs?

We may not have to wait for the terrorists anyway. A six-inch hole burned by boric acid into the head of the Davis-Besse reactor near Toledo, Ohio, recently brought the Great Lakes within three-eighths of an inch of extinction. A tiny, remnant sliver of warped metal may be all that saved millions of people from lethal fallout.

The plant owners want to replace the head. But how do you get it out? Where do you put it once you do? And who's going to volunteer to be exposed to the incredibly intense levels of radiation involved with this horrendous task?

Every week new horrors emerge, from a full-scale fire in California's San Onofre nuclear plant during the deregulation crisis to an endless litany of human errors and mechanical fiascoes that bring us ever-closer to atomic catastrophe.

The first jet that flew into the World Trade Center on September 11 flew directly over the Indian Point nuclear reactors, 40 miles north of New York. Had it dived down a minute earlier, all of New York would now be a radioactive wasteland.

It didn't then, but it could be happening now. George W. Bush may duck what he knew and didn't know on September 11. But we all know plenty about 103 sitting-duck commercial nuclear reactors in the U.S., and the 430-plus worldwide.

Credible threats have been made. The reactors are vulnerable. Their power is not needed. What are we waiting for?

DEALS FOR DUBYA

Trying to make sense of George W. Bush's days in the oil business and his bizarre Harken Energy stock transactions? Well, if you dig deep enough, you'll find a core group of people surrounding the notorious Bank of Credit and Commerce International (aka Bank of Crooks and Criminals International).

BCCI was, among other nefarious things, the bank of choice for Al Qaeda, the CIA, Saddam Hussein and Manuel Noriega. This spooky collection of opium warlords, Arab sheiks, Pakistani financiers and organized crime bosses perpetrated perhaps the greatest banking fraud in world history. BCCI's global criminal conspiracy was aided by connections to Washington insiders like the Bush family, former Secretary of Defense and CIA co-founder Clark Clifford, Senator Orrin Hatch and President Jimmy Carter.

Award-winning journalists Peter Truell and Larry Gurwin document Dubya's ties to Al Qaeda's favorite bank in their authoritative tome, *False Profits: The Inside Story of BCCI, the World's Most Corrupt Financial Empire.*

Truell, a *Wall Street Journal* reporter, and Gurwin, who broke the infamous Banco Ambrosiano scandal in the early 1980s, point out that both Bush political brothers Jeb and Dubya had close links to BCCI. Jeb socialized with Abdur Sakhia, BCCI's Miami branch manager and later the bank's top U.S. official. Jeb's real estate company, Bush Klein Realty, managed the Grove Island complex of luxury condominiums where Sakhia lived. BCCI financed various real estate deals at the complex.

But, as Truell and Gurwin note, "George W. Bush had even closer ties to the BCCI network." In order to understand Bush's bogus Horatio Alger claims of being a struggling West Texas oilman who struck it rich and the later Harken stock shenanigans now in question, people need to look beneath the mythology and political spin.

As three-time Pulitzer Prize nominee Molly Ivins explains, "There's one thing to keep in mind as you read the many stories about George W. in the oil patch… He never found a revenue stream—unless you count investor's dollars flowing from New England to New York into the alkaline West Texas soil."

"The governor's oil-field career can be summed up in a single paragraph. George W. arrived in Midland in 1977, set up a shell company, lost a congressional election in 1978, restarted building the company he'd put on hold, lost more than $2 million of other people's money, and left Midland with $840,000 in his pocket," Ivins offers in *Shrub: The Short But Happy Political Life of George W. Bush.*

Both Ivins and her co-writer Lou Dubose and the tandem of Truell and Gurwin concur that to assess Dubya's dubious business dealings, you've got to understand the role of rich and powerful family friends who were losing money in energy stock investments but speculating in Bush political futures.

When Dubya organized Arbusto Energy Inc. in the 1970s, James R. Bath, a well-known Texas businessman, provided some of the financing. During George Bush senior's tenure as CIA director, the agency allegedly used Bath, a business associate of the Saudi Khalid Bin Mahfouz—described by Truell and Gurwin as a "BCCI insider"—to buy CIA planes from Air America and other secretly held agency airlines.

Public records show that in 1976 the CIA sold several planes to Skyway, a firm managed by Bath. Bath denies it, but his former business partner Bill White has alleged the CIA's role in Skyway in lawsuits and also attested that Bin Mahfouz was an owner of Skyway.

Criminal and civil suits against BCCI established that Bath invested money on Bin Mahfouz's behalf and that he and Bin Mahfouz were part owners of Houston's Main Bank with Ghaith Pharaon, the son of a royal advisor to Saudi Arabia's King Faisal.

Dubya's undercapitalized and floundering Arbusto received badly needed cash from an old Princeton pal of Bush political advisor James Baker, Philip Uzielli, who paid $1 million for a 10 percent share in a company valued at $382,376. "Uzi," who made a fortune in Panama as the CEO of Executive Resources, claims he met Bush senior when he was CIA director.

In the mid 1980s, Arbusto hit hard times and merged with another desperate oil company to form Spectrum 7 Energy Corporation. Harken Energy Corporation, called by *Time* magazine "one of the most mysterious and eccentric outfits ever to drill for oil," rescued Dubya's failing enterprise in a stock swap with Spectrum 7 in 1986. Dubya received nearly $600,000 worth of Harken stock, joined its board of directors and became a $120,000-a-year "consultant" for Harken. The next year, Harken stayed afloat through debt restructuring and was in the same sad financial shape as the earlier Spectrum 7 and Arbusto.

But Harken dramatically reversed its ill fortune in January 1990. As Truell and Gurwin explain, "Harken Energy was awarded one of the most coveted oil deals in the world: a concession to drill for crude oil off the coast of Bahrain. The decision stunned many people in the industry. Harken was not only a small firm, it had never drilled outside the United States, nor had it drilled offshore. The only explanation that made sense to many oil executives, was that the Bahrain government wanted to do a favor for the family of President Bush."

Coincidentally, Bush the Elder enjoyed similar success in the early '60s when his small oil company, Zapata Oil, later listed in a public document as a CIA "asset," received a lucrative contract to drill the first deep-water oil wells off the shores of Kuwait.

Harken's Bahrain deal sharply drove up the price of the company's stock. By June 1990, Dubya had bailed and sold two-thirds of his Harken shares—a transaction he improperly failed to disclose to the Securities and Exchange Commission for several months. Dubya made $318,430 in profit on the sale.

In August, Iraq invaded Kuwait and Harken stock fell by 25 percent, from $4 to $3 a share.

Harken creditors were threatening to foreclose unless debt payments were made, according to *U.S. News and World Report*. "Substantial evidence [existed] to suggest that Bush knew Harken was in dire straits," the magazine reported. Under U.S. law, insiders like Dubya are required to publicly report when they liquidate large blocks of stock. Bush reported his Harken stock sale eight months after the federal deadline, according to the *Wall Street Journal.*

"A extraordinary number of people connected to Harken or the oil deal have ties to BCCI," Truell and Gurwin conclude. In *False Profits,* they document that Harken's investment banking firm Stephens Inc. was the same firm that helped BCCI's founder Agha Hasan Abedi secretly and illegally buy up stock in First American Bank. Bahrian's Prime Minister Sheikh Khalifa bin-Salman al-Khalifa was both a BCCI stockholder in 1990 and instrumental in awarding Harken Bahrain's offshore drilling contract.

Another of Harken's large shareholders was Sheikh Abdullah Taha Bakhsh, whose principal banker was BCCI's Bin Mahfouz. Also, Harken board member Talat Othman, Bakhsh's investment manager, visited the White House on three separate occasions to discuss Middle East policy with President Bush the Elder.

Senator John Kerry's BCCI investigatory committee established that BCCI was a conduit for opium money laundering from the Golden Crescent, where Afghanistan, Iran and Pakistan come together. The Arab oil sheiks were fronts to create the illusion of "petro dollars" funding the bank. Dubya and Harken Energy's friends at BCCI were the core of a group of people—supported by the CIA, the Pakistani Inter-Service Intelligence agency and the Saudi royal family—secretly funding the Al Qaeda terrorist network and Islamic fundamentalist groups in their successful campaign to destroy the Soviet Union.

THE ISSUE IS UNCHECKED POWER

I s the 2002 congressional election the most important in U.S. history? With his TV talk of war, George W. Bush has blown smoke over what's really at stake today: the future of democracy. Not in Iraq—here in the United States.

Never in U.S. history have we been closer to an unchecked one-man, one-party rule than right now. And as the world's sole military superpower, we have made the crisis truly global.

The reality is simple: The right wing of the Republican Party controls three of the four branches of government, and is just a single vote away from taking the fourth.

The executive, the judiciary, the media and the House of Representatives are all in Republican hands. The Senate teeters on the edge. And the USA Patriot Act, passed in the wake of September 11, has obliterated most of the Constitutional guarantees that made this country a democracy in the first place.

Should Congress go Republican in November, there will be no institutional check or balance left to guarantee that the democracy born here two centuries ago will survive.

First, the Republicans control the executive branch, which it took with the first losing candidate in 120 years. Defeated in a popular election by more than 500,000 votes, with many more not properly counted, the administration is firing away with an aggressive far-right agenda that's kept the opposition off balance.

Second, the Republicans control the judicial branch, which formally installed Bush into the presidency, and which is currently dominated by right-wing appointees—many for life—dating back to the Nixon Era.

The Republicans also control the "fourth branch of government." Virtually all major U.S. media is now owned by six corporations. With precious few exceptions, there is no serious debate on the core issues that define American life, and no mainstream coverage of the movements for peace, social justice, environmental, labor, or minority rights to balance the constant blare of right-wing pundits.

All that remains in play—barely—is the Congress. The U.S. House is firmly in control of the Republican right. The minority Democratic opposition is feeble, without strong leadership or direction. Thanks to the defection of Jim Jeffords of Vermont, the Democrats hold a one-vote majority in the U.S. Senate. And that's all that now keeps the far right from total and unchecked control of every branch of the United States government.

To this lethal mix has been added the Patriot Act, virtually obliterating the once-sacred guarantees of the Bill of Rights. Put simply: the executive branch now has the power to arbitrarily brand anyone a "terrorist" with no tangible evidence, and to have that person imprisoned without formal indictment, access to a lawyer or even public notification. Hundreds of unnamed alleged terrorists are thus being held indefinitely in Cuba and perhaps elsewhere with no recourse. If unchecked, such openly contemptuous disregard for the human rights guaranteed in the U.S. Constitution will inevitably spread like a cancer to the core of American liberty and dissent.

The structure of our basic rights is as tenuous under George W. Bush as under many of the Third World dictators installed by his father when he was head of the CIA. Any shred of counter-balance remaining in the system will disappear if the Republicans keep control of the   House and retake the Senate.

Globally, that extends to a Bush Doctrine touting the "right" to intervene in any country, and remove any ruler it does not like, regardless of national sovereignty or international law.

The timing of Bush's latest rhetorical escalation has nothing to do with Iraq. Saddam Hussein is only the latest American-installed enemy of convenience.

This anti-Iraq hysteria is about an aggressive, unelected U.S. regime aiming to complete the coup d'etat it began two years ago.

America's domestic economy is shattered, its stock market in free fall. Unresolved multi-million-dollar scandals still taint Bush from Harken Energy and Vice President Dick Cheney from Halliburton.

Under this regime, joblessness has skyrocketed and the quality of life has plunged. The Bush remedy has been tax breaks for the rich and relentless assaults on organized labor, gays rights, women's rights, minority rights and the natural environment. His foreign policy has been to trash international treaties on atomic testing, missile defense, global warming, international justice and more.

Bush's latest war talk admits to no human or financial cost. He and most of his cabinet are chickenhawks who avoided service in Vietnam. They are selling a videogame war in which Saddam magically disappears with no American bloodshed, no crying widows, parents or orphans. The American veterans suffering from Gulf War I don't exist. Nor does the chaos in Afghanistan left after removing the Taliban and failing to find Osama bin Laden.

A real war against Saddam could cost $100 billion to $200 billion— which the current U.S. economy can't afford. It could destabilize global oil supplies and infuriate much of the Muslim world, 1.2 billion strong. The real costs could include skyrocketing oil prices, economic collapse, and terrorism escalated beyond our wildest nightmares, with the final demise of liberty and peace.

The Republicans are running out the clock on the November election. They are winning their bet against Democrats too timid to oppose a war that has no clothes, and a declaration of global empire with no legs. After that comes an endless procession of Orwellian enemies, conjured at will, a permanent pretext for martial law.

The Harken-Halliburton attack on Iraq is Stage Two of the coup d'etat that began with the installation of an unelected president. It could be completed November 5 with the final capture of the House and Senate.

If that happens, Saddam Hussein will be the least of our worries.

CENTRAL ASIA PIPELINE DIPLOMACY

Following the infamous September 11 terrorist attacks, there's been an active international debate surrounding the Bush administration's secret oil negotiations with the Taliban earlier in the summer of 2001. U.S. oil giant Unocal proposed a massive natural gas pipeline project extracting oil and gas from former Soviet Central Asian republics through then-Taliban ruled Afghanistan to its final destination in Pakistan.

The recently revised and expanded English edition of *Forbidden Truth: U.S.-Taliban Secret Oil Diplomacy and the Failed Hunt For Bin Laden* details the Bush administration's threats against the Taliban a month prior to the tragic September 11 events. French intelligence experts Jean-Charles Brisard and Guillaume Dasquié suggest that Bush administration threats stating that "Either you accept our carpet of gold or we'll carpet you with bombs" led to the attack on the World Trade Center and the Pentagon.

The question of whether secret oil diplomacy led to the terrorist attacks has been ignored in the mainstream U.S. press, but on December 27, 2002, Turkmenistan, Pakistan and Afghanistan signed a framework agreement allowing a $3.2 billion U.S. gas pipeline project to pass through their three countries. Afghan President Harmid Karzai, under the protection of U.S.

special forces serving as his private bodyguards, signed the agreement with the President of Turkmenistan and the Prime Minister of Pakistan.

Karzai is the former consultant for Unocal on the pipeline project that the Taliban refused to allow. An Asian Development Bank (ADB) study outlines how the 950-mile pipeline would bring natural gas reserves from Turkmenistan's Dauletabad fields through Afghanistan to Pakistan. The ADB study lists the Dauletabad as the world's fifth largest gas reserves, according to the website PakNews.com.

Former National Security Advisor Zbigniew Brzezinski, in his 1997 book *The Grand Chessboard,* put forth the thesis that U.S. domination of the globe in the 21st century depended on its control of the Central Asian oilfields. He concluded that unless there was a terrorist attack upon the Unites States, the U.S. people would lack the will to allow our government to seize and control the Central Asian oil and gas deposits in the former Soviet republics.

A 1996 U.S. military "backcasting" exercise on alternative futures hypothesized that a terrorist attack on U.S. soil in the year 2002 would set the stage for U.S. domination of the globe. That scenario was named "Gulliver's Travails."

AN OPEN LETTER TO THE UNITED NATIONS

Recently, U.S. President George W. Bush addressed your august assembly. Despite obtaining his office by what appeared to be a fraudulent coup and stealing the electoral votes of the state of Florida where his brother is governor, he did make one impressive point: "Our principles and our security are challenged today by outlaw groups and regimes that accept no law of morality and have no limit to their violent ambitions."

The UN needs to realize that Bush's statement is a Freudian slip—a self-confession about the real terrorist network that surrounds him in Washington, D.C.

On December 20, 1983, once and future Defense Secretary Donald Rumsfeld traveled to Iraq to extend his hand of friendship to Saddam Hussein. Rumsfeld, then a private citizen, was acting as a liaison for the Reagan administration. As we say in U.S. politics, they knew Saddam was a son-of-a-bitch, but we wanted him as *our* son-of-a-bitch. You know the history here—Somoza, Pappa Doc Duvalier, the Shah of Iran, Marcos, Franco. These are just a few of a long list of fascists and thugs employed by the U.S. to do its imperialist bidding.

Saddam was viewed as just another pawn to settle scores with the Iranian people who had rightfully overthrown that brutal dictator, the

Shah. Just last week, Senator Robert Byrd released documents showing that the U.S. sent biological weapons to its then-friend Saddam throughout the 1980s. This includes anthrax and West Nile virus, among other nasty pathogens.

Also, the U.S.'s trusted British allies sent Saddam anthrax through its lab Porten Down. Never to be left far behind, it is well-documented from the Gulf War that the Germans chipped in by helping to build facilities that could produce chemical weapons for Iraq. Much of this was recently reported in that radical publication *Newsweek*.

Moreover, President Bush had well-established ties to the former Al Qaeda bank of choice, the now-defunct BCCI, the Bank of Credit and Commerce International. You might want to consult the *Wall Street Journal*, which revealed the connections between the BCCI's drugs, arms and terrorist network and Bush's Harken Oil.

Bush's current obsession with Saddam may be to throw us off the trail of his and his father's old buddy Osama bin Laden. As the BBC reported earlier this year, a secret FBI document, numbered 1991 WF213589, from its Washington field office, shows how President Bush removed FBI agents from the bin Laden family trail while the Al Qaeda terrorist network were planning their attacks on the World Trade Center.

The UN needs to look at the strange relationship between Saudi Arabia, Pakistan and the United States. Instead of focusing on whether or not someone from Iraq met once with someone in Al Qaeda, why not look at the obvious? Fifteen of the 19 hijackers were Saudis. One of the masterminds behind the attack, Mohammed Atta, was working for the CIA's ally, the Pakistan Intelligence Service (ISI). More obviously, the U.S. manufactured the Al Qaeda terrorist network, the Saudis financed it, and the Pakistanis trained and recruited its members from the Madressas.

While you're at it, the Security Council might want to delve into the small private company where George Bush the Elder now works, the Carlyle Corporation, which appears to be reaping huge profits from the U.S. military buildup. Instead of worrying whether or not Saddam Hussein is trying to develop a bomb, the Security Council should rather focus on Pakistan, which has developed a nuclear device and recently threatened to use it against India. As the Pulitzer Prize winner Seymour Hersh detailed earlier this year in the *New Yorker*, the United States Special Forces in Afghanistan evacuated Al Qaeda and Pakistani ISI forces to Kashmir.

Terrorist activity soon followed, bringing the world to the brink of nuclear exchange between Pakistan and India.

I would also like to reiterate that the Bush administration is proud of its imperialist plans to dominate the globe and publishes its intentions online. You might want to start with Joint Vision for 2020, which calls for "full spectrum dominance" using space weapons. Also, I recommend an Air Force research paper called "Weather as a force multiplier: Owning the weather in 2025." And before I forget, an April 1996 Air Force research paper, "Alternative futures for 2025: Security planning to avoid surprise," points out how a terrorist attack in the early 21st century would make it possible to galvanize the U.S. people into getting behind Bush's dream of a new Roman empire.

Unless the UN acts now to stop Bush's smiley-faced fascism, we'll have another Hitler on our hands.

PART THREE

THE SUPERPOWER OF PEACE

BUSHLAND, BUSHLAND UBER ALLES

The United Nations Security Council, in all its pompous and hypo-critical glory, passed Resolution 1441 on November 8, 2002. The resolution endorses unrestricted access by weapons inspectors to any sites in Iraq and "warns Iraq that it will face serious consequences" for failure to comply.

Curiously, the UN failed to issue a similar warning to the one country in the world to which Resolution 1441 is most applicable: the United States of America, under the rogue leadership of George W. Bush. The real-ity is, the U.S. has the largest arsenal of weapons of mass destruction in the world, and is the only nation to have used nuclear weapons against civilian populations—twice.

Bush the Lesser, a victim of "dry-drunk syndrome," told America on October 7 that Iraq posed "clear evidence of peril." That very day, CIA Director George Tenet wrote a letter to Congress refuting everything that Bush said.

"Baghdad for now seems to be drawing a line short of conducting ter-rorist attacks or with C.B.W. [chemical or biological warfare] against the United States. Should Saddam conclude that a U.S.-led attack could no longer be deterred he would probably become much less constrained in adopting terrorist actions," Tenet said.

Facing the loss of up to 40 seats in the midterm election, Dubya decided to use Nazi-style propaganda to turn Saddam Hussein, a pan-Arab Baathist, into Osama bin Laden, Saddam's pan-Islamic arch enemy. Luckily for Bush, you can never underestimate the intelligence of the American people. They love to buy the hype, whether it's burgers, malls or athletic footwear fashioned by exploited peasants in the Third World.

In his speech, Bush put forth his new doctrine of "pre-emptive war," which is really an old doctrine that has nothing to do with the situation. "Pre-emptive war" is justified under international law when enemy troops are amassed on your borders ready to attack. Bush obviously hasn't consulted a map or satellite photos. All we've got is two oceans, a friendly Canada and a friendly (if not exploited and polluted) Mexico on our borders. What Bush is really talking about is "preventative war."

Under Bush's doctrine of preventative war, we attack and kill tens of thousands of Iraqis and steal the 110 billion barrels of oil reserve in their ground—because although they don't have nuclear weapons now, or delivery systems for weapons of mass destruction, at some time in the future they may be a threat. I have no doubt that in Bush's mind, he's firmly convinced that Jesus accidentally put that Texas crude under Iraqi soil and he, his father, Dick Cheney and Donald Rumsfeld are entitled to kill as many Arab women and children necessary to get our oil.

The last time the doctrine of preventative war was put forward as a justification for plundering and slaughtering the people of other nations was at the Nuremberg trial by the Nazi leadership. We didn't believe Third Reich propaganda then, we shouldn't believe Fourth Reich propaganda now.

ROGUE NATIONS EXPOSED

To justify the U.S. government's seemingly inevitable invasion and occupation of Iraq, George W. Bush is busy resurrecting the discredited doctrine of "preventative" war—a defense that was last invoked by Nazi party leaders during the Nuremberg trials. Bush's propaganda conveniently ignores our government's plans to seize 119 billion barrels of Iraqi oil. Still, the reality of selling the Iraq war is proving difficult, especially since Iraq has no nuclear weapons and its only known link to biochemical weapons were those supplied by the U.S. and its allies during the 1980s.

Meanwhile, while the U.S. points fingers at Iraq, major media reports have revealed that Bush's chief Islamic ally in the region, Pakistan, provided nuclear technology to North Korea. But apparently Pakistan, a major nuclear power with direct ties to Al Qaeda and North Korean, is not a threat—at least according to Bush.

At Bush's insistence, the United Nations Security Council passed Resolution 1441 on November 8, 2002. A preambulatory clause references "the threat Iraq's noncompliance with Council resolutions and proliferation of weapons of mass destruction and long-range missiles poses to international peace and security."

The resolution stands in sharp contrast to a lack of similar actions that could have been taken against the U.S., Pakistan or the state of Israel, all with well-documented weapons of mass destruction programs.

Iraq complied with the inspections and, as required, provided UN weapons inspectors and the Security Council "with a complete declaration of all aspects of its chemical, biological and nuclear programs."

Phyllis Bennis, fellow at the Institute for Policy Studies, argues that, "This sets Iraq up with a 'damned if you do, damned if you don't' situation. If they claim they have no WMD [weapons of mass destruction] material to declare, Washington will find that evidence of the continuing 'breach' based on the U.S. assertion that Iraq does have viable WMD programs. If Iraq actually declares viable WMD programs, it similarly proves the U.S. claim of continuing breach of Resolution 687."

Richard Perle, chair of the U.S. Defense Policy Board, underscored Bennis' assertion when he confessed to the British Parliament that the U.S. plans to attack Iraq even if UN weapons inspectors gave the country a "clean bill of health," reported Britain's *Mirror* on November 24.

Perle's admission caused Member of Parliament Peter Kilfoyle, a former Defense Minister, to remark, "America is duping the world into believing it supports these inspections. President Bush intends to go to war even if inspections find nothing."

White House Chief of Staff Andrew Card told NBC's *Meet The Press*: "We have the authority by the President's desire to protect and defend the U.S. of America. The U.N. can meet and discuss but we don't need their permission."

With the U.S. and U.K. enforcing a no-fly zone over approximately two-thirds of Iraqi territory, the case for strong action against Iraq remains puzzling.

Bush outlined his case against Saddam Hussein and Iraq to the American people in a televised speech on October 7, 2002. Bush warned of the "clear evidence of peril" if Iraq decided to give chemical and biological weapons to terrorists. Bush did not discuss the perils of the U.S.'s prior policy of giving biological and chemical weapons to Saddam.

On the same day Bush was presenting his charges against Iraq to the American people, CIA Director George Tenet wrote a letter to Congress explaining that "Baghdad for now appears to be drawing a line short of conducting terrorist attacks with conventional or C.B.W. [chemical or biological warfare] against the U.S."

The CIA's former head of counterintelligence told the *London Guardian* that: "Basically, cooked information is working its way into high-level pronouncements and there's a lot of unhappiness about it in intelligence, especially among analysts at the CIA."

Tenet's assessment stands in direct contrast to President Bush's assertion that "Iraq could decide on any given day to provide a biological or chemical weapon to a terrorist group or individual terrorists."

The U.K.'s *Sunday Herald* detailed "Why the CIA Thinks Bush is Wrong," noting that Tenet's October 7 letter specifically spelled out that Bush's invasion policy might have adverse consequences: "Saddam might decide that the extreme step of assisting Islamic terrorists in conducting a WMD attack against the U.S. would be his last chance to exact vengeance by taking a large number of victims with him."

Thus, the new Bush doctrine establishes that any country possessing weapons of mass destruction and possibly motivated to attack another nation at some unforeseen time in the future should be subjected to preventative strikes by the U.S. unilaterally or after failure to comply with a UN Security Council resolution demanding immediate inspections.

Between the September 11, 2001, attacks on the World Trade Center and the Pentagon, and Bush's October 7, 2002, speech, the U.S. had attempted to establish a casus belli for attacking Iraq despite the Bush administration's assertion that the September 11 attacks were perpetrated by Saddam Hussein's sworn enemy and arch-rival, Osama bin Laden and his Al Qaeda network.

Reporter Gary Leupp noted, "First they [the U.S.] seized upon the story, which initially surfaced in a *Newsweek* report on September 19, 2001, that there had been a meeting between hijacker Mohammed Atta and Iraqi intelligence officers, including Farouk Hijaze, Iraq's ambassador to Turkey in Prague in June of 2000."

Leupp points out that had not "both British and Czech intelligence services" publicly "refuted" the story, the U.S. may have had justification for retaliating against Iraq. Moreover, Leupp suggests that the early U.S. attempts to link the anthrax attack to Iraqi laboratories, later discounted, was the U.S. in search of a cause, any cause, for war.

Francis A. Boyle, a University of Illinois professor of law, points out, "There is no evidence that Iraq was involved in the events on September

11.... They are fishing around for some other justification to go to war with Iraq. They have come up with the doctrine of preemptive attack."

Boyle notes that the doctrine of preemptive attack "was rejected by the Nuremberg tribunal" after lawyers for Nazi defendants used it to defend the actions of Germany's Third Reich.

James Rubin, the Assistant Secretary of State during the Clinton administration, analyzed the dangers of President Bush's new national security strategy in October 2002. He wrote: "The problem with the Bush document is that it appears to make first strikes the rule rather than the exception."

While the Bush administration stressed its multilateralism by pointing to the UN Security Council's Resolution 1441, the *New York Times* reported that prior to the adoption of the resolution, U.S. pilots were already bombing southern Iraq on practice runs.

The *Times* reported, "Now, the Navy pilots gain combat experience when they police the no-flight zone. They have the chance to practice bombing tactics when the Iraqis refrain from firing at the patrols and to hone their skills in case of war."

With such U.S. tactics, it's not surprising that the *Washington Post* reported that "Fear of U.S. Power Shapes Iraq Debate."

In August 2002, a Knight Ridder article disclosed that Defense Secretary Donald Rumsfeld's staff had created a special planning unit for the invasion of Iraq. The story detailed how Deputy Secretary of Defense Paul Wolfowitz was working with a group primarily composed of civilians to launch an invasion of Iraq.

"The Bush administration began its campaign for a new resolution at about the same time it unveiled its national security doctrine, which outlines the concept of preemptive action to counter perceived threats," according to the *Washington Post*. "The new doctrine unnerved even close allies who feared that the world's only superpower no longer felt bound by the international rules established after World War II."

By applying the Bush administration's new doctrine of preemptive military strikes, a strong case can be made that the UN Security Council needs to take action against the U.S. First, there's ample evidence that the U.S. government or its intelligence apparatus created and protected Osama bin Laden prior to the September 11 attacks.

Professor Michael Chossudovsky, a bin Laden biographer and Director of the Centre for Research on Globalization, holds that, "Lost in the barrage of recent history, the role of the CIA in supporting and developing international terrorist organizations during the Cold War and its aftermath is casually ignored or downplayed by the Western media."

Richard Labeviere echoes these sentiments in his book *Dollars for Terror: The U.S. and Islam.* Relying heavily on European intelligence sources, Labeviere argues that the Al Qaeda network was "nurtured and encouraged by the U.S. intelligence community, especially during the Clinton years." He further asserts that bin Laden "was protected because the network was designed to serve U.S. foreign policy and military interests."

By taking a broader geostrategic approach, Labeviere contends that, "The policy of guiding the evolution of Islam and of helping them against our adversaries worked marvelously well in Afghanistan against the Red Army. The same doctrines can still be used to destabilize what remains of Russian power, and especially to counter the Chinese influence in Central Asia."

Did the U.S. turn a blind eye to pre-September 11 warning signs that this policy could backfire? The authoritative *Jane's Intelligence Digest* reported that, "Back in March [2001], Moscow's Permanent Mission at the UN submitted to the UN Security Council an unprecedentedly detailed report on Al Qaeda's terrorist infrastructure in Afghanistan but the U.S. government opted not to act."

The French daily *Le Figaro* (ironically owned by U.S. defense contractor the Carlyle Group, which employs former president George H.W. Bush), reported in October 2001 that Osama bin Laden received treatment at the American hospital in Dubai, one of the United Arab Emirates, in July 2001. Moreover, *Le Figaro* reported that bin Laden met with a top CIA official while being treated at the American hospital.

The *Le Figaro* article raises the question of how bin Laden, eligible for execution for his alleged attacks on the *U.S.S. Cole* and the deaths of U.S. sailors, could reportedly fly out of Dubai on a private jet with no Navy fighters waiting to force him down and take him into custody.

The *Toronto Star* suggested, "One possible conclusion is that the bin Laden terror problem was allowed to get out of hand because bin Laden, himself, had powerful protectors in both Washington and Saudi Arabia."

There's enough evidence for the Security Council to investigate U.S. ties to bin Laden and Al Qaeda as well as to look into whether the U.S. Department of Defense was planning a preemptive strike against Iraq before any legal basis was established under international law. By Bush administration standards, the U.S. may have created a precedent that could be later used against itself for its long-standing relationships with bin Laden—relationships that reportedly continued until less than two months before the September 11 terrorist attacks.

The Security Council might also want to apply the terms of Resolution 1441 to any other nation that has participated in Iraq's chemical and biological program in the past—a nation like the United States.

In September 2002, U.S. Senator Robert C. Byrd, a Democrat from West Virginia, went public with documents obtained from the federal government establishing the United States' role in the development of Iraq's biochemical program in the 1980s. Byrd told the *Charleston Gazette*, "We have in our hands the equivalent of a Betty Crocker cookbook of ingredients that the U.S. allowed Iraq to obtain and that may well have been used to concoct biological weapons."

Between 1985 and 1988, following the approval of the U.S. government, the nonprofit American Type Culture Collection sent 11 shipments to Iraq that included anthrax, botulinum toxin and gangrene. Also, between January 1980 and October 1993, the U.S. Centers for Disease Control shipped a variety of biological and toxic specimens to Iraq, including West Nile virus and Dengue fever, according to the *Gazette*.

Senator Byrd's release of information followed statements from Secretary of Defense Donald Rumsfeld that he had no knowledge of any such shipments in testimony before the Arms Services Committee.

In 1984, a United Nations report alleged that chemical weapons had been used by Iraq against Iran. The *New York Times* reported from Baghdad that, then-former Secretary of State Donald Rumsfeld was in Iraq as an envoy for President George H.W. Bush. The *Times* wrote, "American diplomats pronounced themselves satisfied with relations between Iraq and the U.S. and suggest that normal diplomatic ties have been restored in all but name."

U.S. Representative Dennis Kucinich, a Democrat from Ohio, wrote that "During the administration of Ronald Reagan, 60 helicopters were sold to Iraq. Later reports said Iraq used U.S.-made helicopters to spray Kurds with chemical weapons. According to the *Washington Post*, Iraq used mustard gas against Iran with the help of intelligence from the CIA."

In a forthcoming paper in the scientific journal *Bulletin of Atomic Scientists*, Professor of International Security Malcolm Dando and Mark Wheelis, a microbiologist, put forth the thesis that U.S. actions are undermining the 1972 biological weapons conventions in order to continue secret U.S. research on biological weapons. "They also point to the paradox of the U.S. developing such weapons at a time when it is proposing military action against Iraq on the grounds that Iraq is breaking international treaties," wrote the *Guardian* in a preview of the forthcoming article.

The U.S. has the world's most extensive arsenal of chemical, biological and nuclear weapons. Under the terms of Resolution 1441, there's more than enough evidence to merit a UN inspection of U.S. sites, and investigate the U.S.'s role in Iraq's weapons of mass destruction programs.

FITRAKIS

January 26, 2003

IMPEACH PRESIDENT BUSH

In the last few months, evidence has mounted to warrant the impeachment of President George W. Bush. Congressional authorities take note—he must be stopped before he can commit additional high crimes and misdemeanors against America and the world.

First, there's Bush's strange relationship with a bizarre little company in Lansing, Michigan, known as Bioport. The company, despite failing various FDA inspections and being accused of bad record-keeping, holds the only federal contract for producing the anthrax vaccine. Bush has rewarded Bioport with favors such as ongoing military protection, and within weeks of September 11 granted Bioport a contract that tripled the price per vaccine.

Owners and investors in Bioport include former Chairman of Joint Chiefs of Staff William Crowe and Fuad El-Hibri. Public records and foreign press reports have linked El-Hibri to the selling of anthrax to Saudi Arabia after the Pentagon refused to. He's also a business associated of the bin Laden family. A real congressional investigation of Bush's relationships with the bin Laden family, El-Hibri and the related drug bank BCCI would easily lead to the President's impeachment.

Second, the President's utter contempt for U.S. citizens was displayed in his appointments of three criminals: the pompous pipe-puffing Admiral John Poindexter, Elliott Abrams of Iran-Contra infamy and wanted war criminal Henry Kissinger.

Poindexter, who now runs the Office of Total Information Awareness, is busily keeping files on every U.S. citizen. Well, put this in your file on Poindexter: He supervised the illegal arms for hostage sale to Iran that violated the Arms Export Control Act; he sanctioned the funneling of profits from that illegal sale into the Nicaraguan Contras, a group more famous for its drug-running than fighting the Sandinistas; he lied about his activities and destroyed evidence during the congressional investigation; and a federal jury found him guilty of lying and obstructing justice. But the fix was apparently in and two conservative federal appeals judges overturned his convictions.

After lying to Congress about the Iran-Contra scandal and being convicted on two counts, Abrams was pardoned by Bush the Elder. Now thanks to Bush the Lesser, he is the top Middle East advisor on the National Security Council.

And what can we say about Kissinger? From the "secret bombings" of Cambodia to the overthrow of Chile's democracy, there is perhaps no figure more hated in the world than the good doctor. This did not stop Dubya from appointing him to cover up the real causes of September 11. Fortunately, Special K was forced to resign when he refused to disclose his clients from his private "consulting firm," Kissinger and Associates. We would have stood a better chance of getting to the truth of September 11 had we dug up the bones of Earl Warren and created another bogus Warren Commission.

Meanwhile, the forces of Big Oil surrounding Bush are hell-bent on stealing the Iraqi people's petroleum. Somehow they seem able to convince Americans that Baby Jesus himself put that oil in Iraq for us to pilfer in the name of God and country.

Despite Dubya's best efforts to hide the crucial role of Bush Senior in arming Iraq with biochemical weapons in the 1980s—including Secretary of State Colin Powell's bullying the UN into allowing him to remove 8,000 key pages of Iraq's 12,000-page dossier on weapons—the story continues to break.

Finally, Dubya's foreign policy contains the rabid elements of inbred elitist ignorance. A week before Christmas, Human Rights Watch reported that the U.S. military violated international law in Afghanistan by indiscriminately dropping cluster bombs in civilian areas. That same week, the Bush administration announced a new strategy of covert actions and pre-emptive strikes, including nukes, against any country that dares attack U.S. troops now stationed in at least 148 nations throughout the world.

The President also announced his new version of Star Wars, guaranteeing huge profits for the U.S. military-industrial complex and insuring we will continue to be the nation with the greatest stockpile of weapons of mass destruction.

A REGIME THAT HATES DEMOCRACY CAN'T FIGHT FOR IT

George W. Bush says he wants to attack Iraq to install democracy. But as he explained on December 18, 2000: "If this were a dictatorship, it'd be a heck of a lot easier, just so long as I'm the dictator."

Under Bush the constitutional guarantees that have made America a beacon to the world for two centuries have been shredded in two short years. In terms of basic legal rights and sanctuary from government spying, Americans may be less free under President George II than as British subjects under King George III in 1776.

Though the trappings of free speech remain on the surface of American society, the Homeland Security Act, USA Patriot Act and other massively repressive legislation, plus Republican control of the executive, legislative and judicial branches, plus GOP dominance of the mass media, have laid the legal and political framework for a totalitarian infrastructure which, when combined with the capabilities of modern computer technology, may be unsurpassed.

The administration has used the terrorist attack of September 11, 2001, as pretext for this centralization of power. But most of it was in the works long before September 11 as part of the war on drugs and Bush's modus operandi as the most secretive and authoritarian President in U.S. history.

So with today's U.S. as a model, what would be in store for Iraqis should Bush kill thousands of them to replace Saddam Hussein?

• President Bush has asserted the right to execute "suspected terrorists" without trial or public notice.

• The administration claims the right to torture "suspected terrorists," and by many accounts has already done so.

• Attorney General John Ashcroft has asserted the right to brand "a terrorist" anyone he wishes without evidence or public hearing or legal recourse.

• The administration has arrested and held without trial hundreds of "suspected terrorists" while denying them access to legal counsel or even public notification that they have been arrested.

• The administration has asserted the right to inspect the records of bookstores and public libraries to determine what American citizens are reading.

• The administration has asserted the right to break into private homes and tap the phones of U.S. citizens without warrants.

• The administration has attempted to install a neighbors-spying-on-neighbors network that would have been the envy of Joe Stalin.

• The administration has effectively negated the Freedom of Information Act and runs by all accounts the most secretive regime in U.S. history.

• When the General Accounting Office, one of the few reliably independent federal agencies, planned to sue Vice President Dick Cheney to reveal who he met to formulate the Bush Energy Plan, Bush threatened to slash GAO funding, and the lawsuit was dropped.

• After losing the 2000 election by more than 500,000 popular votes, the administration plans to control all voting through computers operated by just three companies, with code that can be easily manipulated, as may have been done in Georgia in 2002, winning seats for a Republican governor and U.S. senator, and in Nebraska to elect and re-elect U.S. Senator Chuck Hagel, an owner of the voting machine company there.

• FCC Chair Michael Powell (son of the Secretary of State) is enforcing the administration's demand that regulation be ended so nearly all mass media can be monopolized by a handful of huge corporations.

• Attorney General Ashcroft has assaulted states' rights, a traditional Republican mainstay, using federal troops to trash public referenda legalizing medical marijuana in nine states.

• Ashcroft has overridden his own federal prosecutors and assaulted local de facto prohibitions against the death penalty, which has been renounced by every other industrial nation and is now used only by a handful of dictatorships, including Iraq.

Overseas, the U.S. record is infamous. Among those it has put into power are Saddam Hussein, the Taliban and Manuel Noriega, not to mention Somoza, Pinochet, Marcos, Mobutu, the Shah, the Greek Junta and too many other murderous dictators to mention in a single article.

Afghanistan, leveled in the name of democracy and the hunt for Osama bin Laden, now stands ruined and abandoned. In sequel, Bush is gathering Iraq attackers with the promise of cash bribes, oil spoils and conquered land.

Turkey, Bulgaria and Bush's manufactured Iraqi opposition are already squabbling over the booty. Bush says rebuilding will be funded by Iraqi oil revenues, probably administered through the same core regime now in place, but with a different figurehead.

In other words, the media hype about bringing democracy to Iraq is just that. There is absolutely no reason to believe a U.S. military conquest would bring to Iraq the beloved freedoms George W. Bush is so aggressively destroying here in America. A regime that so clearly hates democracy at home is not about to wage war for one abroad.

WASSERMAN & FITRAKIS
March 4, 2003

AMERICA'S WILLING EXECUTIONERS

I f he launches an attack on Iraq without the approval of the United Nations Security Council, George W. Bush will be guilty of crimes on par with those committed by the infamous Nazi leaders who were tried at Nuremberg after World War II. The law is clear. At Nuremberg, American, British, French and Soviet jurists used international conventions, legal precedent and a global moral consensus to establish a code of conduct deemed the standard for all nations.

Key was the "crimes against humanity" prohibition stemming from the conscious slaughter of six million Jews, leftists, gypsies and others by the Nazi fanatics.

But also crucial was the ban on unprovoked attack by one nation against another. The explosive fuse that set off World War II was the September 1, 1939, Nazi attack on Poland, which was unprovoked by any stretch of the military imagination. By all accounts it was an act of aggression and conquest, which led ultimately to as many as 50 million deaths over the next six years.

Article VI of the Nuremberg Charter defines "Crimes Against Peace" as "planning, preparation, initiation or waging of war of aggression, or a war in violation of international treaties...or participation in a common plan or conspiracy...to wage an aggressive war."

A week before the unprovoked Nazi assault on Poland, Hitler promised his generals he would provide "a propagandistic reason for starting the war." He then justified a "preemptive" strike based on lies about a non-existent Polish Army attack against Germany.

The Nazi attack date had been set for more than a year. "The victor will not be asked afterwards whether he told the truth or not," Hitler told his generals. "In starting and waging a war it is not right that matters, but victory."

After Hitler's deceptions were revealed at Nuremberg, the surviving Nazis based their defense on the claim of "preventative war," claiming a need to protect Germany from an impending Polish attack. They were the last—until Bush—to use that rationale.

It didn't work. Ranking Nazi commandants, starting with Hermann Goering, Hitler's number two, were convicted and sentenced to death. The charge of invading Poland—and that alone—was deemed sufficient to warrant hanging.

Unless Saddam Hussein launches an attack on the United States very soon, any American attack on Iraq without UN approval would be on a legal par with the Nazi attack on Poland.

A key U.S. argument, that Iraq was somehow linked to the September 11 terror attacks, has been definitively dismissed. In the 18 months since, all credible evidence points to intense hostility rather than cooperation between Al Qaeda and Saddam Hussein. Colin Powell, arguing in front of the UN, failed to prove any cooperative connection.

Iraq has been ordered to disarm by the United Nations, whose legal legitimacy was essential to the 1991 campaign that drove Saddam out of Kuwait.

Thus far, there is no UN consensus that the Iraqis have failed to comply with the terms of that defeat to an extent that would justify a renewed military attack—one that would inevitably involve civilian casualties.

With no claim of having been attacked, Bush has instead argued that his war on Iraq would be "preemptive," meant to prevent Saddam from launching a future war. But Iraq has not attacked anyone in more than 12 years, and two-thirds of the country is under a no-fly zone. Thus Bush is merely resurrecting the preventative war doctrine invoked by the Nazis before their Nuremberg hangings.

In 1953 President Dwight Eisenhower, the former Supreme Allied Commander, dismissed the idea of a preventative war against the Soviet Union. "All of us have heard this term 'preventive war' since the earliest days of Hitler," he said. "I don't believe there is such a thing; and, frankly, I wouldn't even listen to anyone seriously that came in and talked about such a thing."

Bush has now added to the list of pre-war demands a "regime change" by which Saddam would give up power. Bush then proposes rebuilding Iraq along democratic lines.

But Nazi functionaries at Nuremberg also received stiff sentences for approving essentially the same totalitarian statutes that now appear in the Homeland Security and Patriot Acts authorizing secret arrest, detention and "disappearances" of American citizens without legal recourse or public notification. At Nuremberg, such laws were recognized as a form of state terror.

The embrace of such laws in America casts serious doubt on the Bush administration's real willingness to install democracy anywhere else.

When the Nazis attacked Poland in 1939, no one envisioned that just eight years later Germany would be leveled and its all-powerful reichmarshals would be tried and sentenced under international law.

Such a vision seems less far-fetched today. America's current military might has prompted the Bush administration to frame its proposed war in terms of a "crusade" against "evil." But military action against Iraq is guaranteed to inflame the passions of 1.2 billion Muslims. The proposed war is explicitly opposed by the Pope. International support is extremely limited. The U.S. itself is deeply divided, with its economy in serious trouble.

The diplomatic campaign for this attack has been handled with all the wisdom and foresight of madmen lighting matches in a room full of gasoline. There is no reason to expect a military campaign would be handled any better.

It is clear from the precedents at Nuremberg that any American attack on Iraq without United Nations approval would be illegal under international law. It is also clear that the inevitable civilian casualties resulting from such an attack would qualify as crimes against humanity.

And sooner or later, the American perpetrators of such an attack and related crimes might well find themselves standing trial before some sort of Nuremberg-style international tribunal.

Given such circumstances, the guilt of George W. Bush will not be in doubt. But the guilt of subordinates giving supporting orders, and of soldiers and functionaries carrying them out, will also be a given.

The Nuremberg court, including its American judges, repeatedly ruled that those who "only followed orders" in committing atrocities were guilty of crimes against humanity.

America's executioners who "only follow orders" in perpetrating this illegal attack on Iraq should understand that they stand to be found just as guilty as the ones giving those orders. And that one way or another, sooner or later, that guilt will demand payment.

IS BUSH PLAYING A SHELL GAME WITH THE UN AND IRAQ?

H as the Bush administration suckered the United Nations into weakening Iraq prior to a pre-meditated murderous attack? The facts are these:

• Bush's original stance was that the United Nations must force Iraq to disarm, in keeping with treaties signed after Iraq's 1991 defeat after invading Kuwait. His charges that Iraq had failed to honor these promises led the UN to force Iraq to further disarm.

• According to the official report of UN weapons inspectors, as delivered on March 7, 2003, by Hans Blix, Iraq has made "significant" steps toward disarming, among other things destroying many of its missiles.

• According to additional reports, Iraq may have destroyed most or all of its chemical and biological weapons early in the 1990s.

• According to most credible reports, Iraq does not have the near-term ability to build nuclear weapons.

In short, by all internationally accepted standards, Iraq has moved toward significant compliance with the formal demands of the UN, and cannot be considered a credible threat to the United States.

At the behest of the UN, Iraq has significantly weakened its ability to defend its citizens from mass slaughter by an attacking superpower.

But George W. Bush says just such a mass slaughter may come no matter what the UN Security Council or its weapons inspectors say about Iraq's compliance with the UN's—and Bush's—original demands.

At his press conference on March 6, Bush dictated a new requirement for avoiding mass slaughter on which the UN never voted, and which was never formally presented to the Iraqis: Saddam Hussein must go.

Should Bush attempt to enforce this demand with violence, he will have used the United Nations—and Iraqi compliance with UN mandates—in a shell game to diminish the Iraqis' ability to defend themselves.

Such a move would rank as one of the most cynical ploys ever used by a world leader. It would forever pollute the reputation of the United States. It would permanently cripple if not destroy the peace-keeping ability of the United Nations.

There's little doubt Saddam may well have more to hide. He is a violent dictator, like dozens of others the U.S. has installed in victim nations over the decades.

But Bush's homeland contempt for the Bill of Rights and other constitutional guarantees of personal freedom, privacy and human rights makes suspect the kind of "democracy" he might bring to a conquered Iraq.

Through the Project for a New American Century and other right-wing think tanks, key Bush cohorts such as Donald Rumsfeld and Paul Wolfowitz, have long demanded a "regime change" in Iraq that would lead to U.S. hegemony over Arab oil reserves. Iraq would be the first Middle Eastern "domino" to fall definitively under direct U.S. control.

But in 1996, Bush's father, former President George H.W. Bush, warned that "to occupy Iraq would instantly shatter our coalition, turning the whole Arab world against us, and make a broken tyrant into a latter-day Arab hero."

Former Defense Secretary Dick Cheney, now Dubya's Vice President, later said that a war in the streets of Baghdad "would have put large numbers of Iraqi civilians and hundreds of thousands of our troops at risk of being killed."

Cheney added in 1997 that finding Saddam was worth "not very many" American lives. "The only way to make certain you could get him was to go occupy all of Iraq and start sorting through Iraqis until you find Saddam Hussein."

Last year Secretary of State Colin Powell warned Dubya that an attack on Iraq without strong global support could be "much more complicated and bloody" than the first Gulf War.

That might be the understatement of the new millennium. UN weapons inspectors have increased Iraq's vulnerability to martial conquest. Through bait-and-switch, Bush has used the UN and its members as instruments of a military agenda they have not approved.

It's hard to imagine the global firestorm of revulsion and fury that would explode should Bush now use the advantage they've given him to kill Iraqi citizens for regional hegemony, as he clearly intended to do all along.

ANOTHER SICK CAESAR

I t's time for U.S. citizens to demand that President George W. Bush's cabinet invoke Section Four of the 25th Amendment and remove him from office. By a majority vote of the cabinet and the Vice President, transmitted in writing to both the Speaker of the House and the President Pro Tempore of the Senate, the President may be declared "unable to discharge the powers and duties of his office."

Increasingly, journalists and mental health professionals are willing to admit that the cognitively impaired President may indeed be mentally ill.

What else would drive a President who lost an election by 500,000 votes to attack the arch-enemy of Osama bin Laden, Saddam Hussein, rather than to pursue the September 11 terrorists in the Al Qaeda network? What would cause a President to ignore his generals, his own intelligence agencies, the major religious leaders of the world and the vast majority of the world's people in pursuing an unnecessary and destabilizing war that is likely to plunge the world into chaos for the next hundred years?

But while there's growing concern that the President is mentally disturbed, there's no consensus as to his actual illness.

Dr. Carol Wolman asked the question "Is the 'President' Nuts?" on the website Counterpunch.org. In an attempt to analyze Bush's bizarre behavior, putting "the world on a suicidal path," Wolman suggests the President may be suffering from antisocial personality disorder, as described in the *Diagnostic and Statistical Manual of Mental Illnesses.* As the manual points out, "There is a pervasive pattern of disregard for and violation of the rights of others: 1) failure to conform to social norms with respect to lawful behaviors as indicated by repeatedly performing acts that are grounds for arrest; 2) deceitfulness, as indicated by repeated lying... 5) reckless disregard for safety of self or others."

Professor Katherine Van Wormer, co-author of the authoritative *Addiction Treatment,* worries about Bush's brain chemistry following some 20 years of alcohol addiction and alleged illicit drug use. Van Wormer notes that "George W. Bush manifests all the classic patterns of what alcoholics in recovery call 'the dry drunk.' His behavior is consistent with being brought on by years of heavy drinking and possible cocaine use."

Alan Bisbort echoes Van Wormer's theory in the *American Politics Journal,* in an article titled "Dry Drunk: Is Bush Making a Cry for Help?"

The list of possible madnesses afflicting King George goes on and on. Some suggest paranoia, obsessive-compulsive disorder, narcissistic personality disorder, religious delusions and depression.

Former National Security Agency employee-turned-investigative journalist Wayne Madsen noted that the President was slurring his speech during the State of the Union address.

Perhaps more shocking is the title of Maureen Dowd's March 9, 2003, *New York Times* column, "Xanax Cowboy." Dowd's lead read: "As he rolls up to America's first pre-emptive invasion, bouncing from motive to motive, Mr. Bush is trying to sound rational, not rash. Determined not to be petulant, he seemed tranquilized."

Of course many Americans will reject the notion that the President—with an estimated 91 I.Q., who could not name crucial Middle East leaders during his campaign—could be mentally unstable. Few realize that this has been a common problem with past presidents.

Jim Cannon, an aide to incoming Reagan administration Chief of Staff Howard Baker, suggested in a March 1987 memo that President Reagan was incapable of performing his duties. Analyzing Reagan's behavior, Cannon wrote, "He was lazy; he wasn't interested in the job. They say he won't read the papers they gave him—even short position papers and documents. They say he won't come over to work—all he wanted to do was watch movies and television at the residence." Cannon recommended the administration consider invoking the 25th Amendment to remove Reagan.

In retrospect, we know that Reagan was in the early stages of Alzheimer's disease; it was apparent to many political scientists and journalists at the time, who frequently commented on Reagan's mistaking fictional movies for real historical events.

The images of Richard Nixon wandering around the White House drunk, asking a portrait of Abe Lincoln for advice, are forever immortalized in Woodward and Bernstein's *The Final Days*. Luckily in Nixon's case, National Security Advisor Henry Kissinger and Chief of Staff General Alexander Haig took control to make sure the President would not launch a pre-emptive war or nuclear attack, or order a military coup to stop the impeachment.

Since the United States, if it indulges Bush's apparent madness, will embark on a course similar to imperial Rome, historical analogies may be found in Michael Grant's book *Sick Caesars: Madness and Malady in Imperial Rome*. Searching through the text, the comparisons between Rome's inbred elite families and the out-of-touch Bush dynasty are obvious.

What's harder to determine is which sick Caesar Bush most emulates. Comparing him to Caligula prior to an attack on Iraq would be unfair, although historian A.A. Barrett noted that an eyewitness described Caligula as "a fidgety neurotic." Barrett writes, "Though his behavior perhaps fell short of madness, it is impossible to determine the degree of rationality he retained."

Caligula has been labeled as "epileptic, schizoid, schizophrenic or just chronically alcoholic." There's no evidence that President Bush has ever had epilepsy; other than that, the Caligula analogy does fit.

A case can be made for comparing Claudius to "I, Dubya." As Grant explains, Claudius' ailments included "meningitis, poliomyelitis, pre-natal encephalitis, multiple sclerosis, alcoholism and congenital cerebral paralysis."

Except for the last two diagnoses, it's not an exact fit. However, as one Roman recorded, "Claudius was, or was looked upon, as the idiot which he was sometimes made out to be.... He was far from normal."

Some may suggest a comparison to Commodus. As Grant writes, "Physically, at least he was well proportioned. [However] his expression was vacant as is usual with drunkards, and his speech disordered." Bush is a recovering alcoholic with a speech disorder, in need of therapy, though not a current alcohol abuser. Thus, the search continues.

Finally, after much investigation, Bush is nearly a perfect match for the lesser known Caracalla. As Grant describes it, "Caracalla was always pushed forward by his father, who although he realized his defects possessed, like most emperors, [supported] strong dynastic ideas. His younger brother Geta [read: Jeb], was also pushed forward, although more slowly."

My favorite passage is this: "For he [Caracalla] was sick not only in body, partly from visible and partly from secret ailments, but in mind as well, suffering from certain distressing visions, and often he thought he was being pursued by his father, and by his brother, armed with swords."

But, another section suggests that Bush may actually be the reincarnation of Caracalla: "Though it is at least certain that he was not only intemperate but had appalling nerves and nervous hallucinations, which made him very restless (not inactive) and all the more emphatic in his distaste for everyone except his soldiers. This meant that he could be judged as a criminal rather than a lunatic."

One historian's assessment of Caracalla is so strikingly similar to Bush, it sends chills: "His mind became unbalanced. His habitual mood of sullen and suspicious moroseness would sharpen into a craving for bloodshed which the slaughter of the arena [read: Texas' Death Row] could not appease, and which would drive him into a homicidal fury in which revengefulness appears to have been confusedly combined with religious and moral motives."

Thankfully, Grant tells us that Caracalla's "short reign was a joke. A bad joke at that."

By invoking the 25th Amendment, we can make Emperor Bush's reign equally short. The problem, of course, is that we would be left with Vice President Dick Cheney, who may be even more disturbed than the President. Et tu, Cheney?

THE EMERGING SUPERPOWER OF PEACE

A midst the agonizing crisis over Iraq, the violent contortions of the world's only military superpower have given birth to a transcendental force: the global SuperPower of Peace.

That George W. Bush's obsession with Saddam Hussein has become a global issue at all is perhaps the most tangible proof of this new superpower's potential clout.

Only one thing has slowed Bush from launching his attack against Iraq: the economic, political, moral and spiritual power of an intangible human network determined to stop this war.

Bush has amassed the most powerful killing machine humankind has ever created. He's set its fuse on the borders of an impoverished desert nation with no credible ability to protect itself. His military henchmen believe the conquest of this small country can be done quickly, with relatively few casualties on the attacking side (though many civilians would die on the Iraqi side, as they did in the 1991 Gulf War).

The potential prizes are enormous:

• Outright control of the world's second-largest oil reserve.

• Removal of Bush's hated personal rival, a U.S.-installed despot gone bad.

• A pivotal military base in the heart of the Middle East.

• Hugely lucrative contracts for both the destroyers and the rebuilders of Iraq.

• The opportunity to test a new generation of ultra high-tech weaponry, display its awesome killing power and demonstrate a willingness to use that power.

• The fulfillment of Biblical prophesy as seen through the eyes of religious fanatics.

But after months of preparation, the world's only military superpower has hesitated. Instead of obliterating Baghdad—as it could at any moment—the Bush cabal has flinched.

Defense Secretary Donald Rumsfeld says he needs no military allies. But he's desperately courting them. Bush says he doesn't need UN approval. But he's desperately sought it.

Why? One could argue the U.S. has been marking time because it's not quite ready, with deployments and other technical needs not yet met.

But all that is now far more difficult with an astounding rejection by Turkey, which shares a strategic border with Iraq. Turkish opposition to war is running a fierce 80 to 90 percent. Major arm-twisting (and a $26 billion bribe) has not bought permission to use Turkish land and air space.

Meanwhile, the "no" votes of China, Russia, France and Germany represent the official opinion of some two billion people. They are irrelevant to the mechanics of armed conquest.

But the four naysayers represent enormous political and economic power. So do scores of other nations whose nervous millions now march for peace.

"Never before in the history of the world has there been a global, visible, public, viable, open dialogue and conversation about the very legitimacy of war," says Robert Muller, a long-time UN guiding light who views this global resistance as virtually miraculous.

To all this has been added the opposition of the Pope. The Bush cabal may be asking that infamous question: "How many divisions does the Pope have?"

Meanwhile, the spiritual opposition has been joined by a wide spectrum of religious organizations, including Bush's own church. Though constantly speaking in religious terms, Bush has refused to meet with the broad range of clerics who oppose his war.

Specific corporations, such as Dick Cheney's Halliburton and Richard Perle's consulting firm, stand to make a fortune from Gulf War II. But mainstream financial and commercial institutions are understandably terrified.

The American economy is already staggering under deep recession. Bush's tax cuts will yield stratospheric deficits for decades to come. The U.S. economy now bears the sickly pallor of a collapsing empire.

China counts a billion-plus citizens and a rapidly emerging economic powerhouse. France and Germany dominate the European Union, which will soon outstrip the U.S. in gross output and consumer spending. A billion-plus Muslims must also be accounted for.

Tragically, violent terrorism might also accompany a Bush attack. In bloodshed and degraded quality of life, the cost would be horrifying. The U.S. airline industry has already warned it might not survive another round of terrorism. That's probably a tiny tip of the economic iceberg.

Through the Internet, the nonviolent movement is linked by billions of e-mails and forwarded articles meant to surround and circumvent the corporate media. They warn the bloodshed in this proposed war would be unconscionable. That its ecological costs would be unsustainable. That civil rights and liberties are being trashed. And that the multiplier effects of such devastating chaos cannot be predicted.

A war between unelected macho madmen, launched by a military superpower against its own puppet gone astray, is the ultimate yin to the new movement's yang.

If, as you read this, war has broken out, know this: the global SuperPower of Peace can bend, but it won't break.

If Bush still hasn't attacked, and Saddam continues to be disarmed, count another day the SuperPower of Peace has extended its pre-emptive influence, its maturity, its scope.

No matter what ultimately happens in Iraq, the new millennium will be neither American nor Chinese nor European nor military nor corporate nor dictatorial. It belongs to the SuperPower of Peace, being born before our electronic eyes.

A PLEA TO LAURA BUSH TO ASSUME THE PRESIDENCY

For the third time in U.S. history, the wife of the President must step forward and assume the powers of the office. We plead with Laura Bush to take over the reins of the White House at this most crucial and dangerous moment.

Such a radical step is warranted when the President himself is mentally incapable of handling the job. It happened when Edith Wilson took over for her husband Woodrow, who suffered a stroke. It happened again when Nancy Reagan took over for her husband Ronald, who may have been in the preliminary stages of Alzheimer's disease. It has now happened again, as Laura Bush must take over from her husband George, who is clearly delusional and may be in a manic state involving alcohol, Xanax or other drugs.

Under normal circumstances one might assume that the Vice President would assume power. In this case, Dick Cheney is ineligible because of a clear conflict of interest. Halliburton, the company which paid him $35 million when he left its presidency to run for national office, still pays Cheney $1 million per year. But Halliburton also stands to make a huge amount of money destroying and then rebuilding Iraq.

Cheney, of course, should resign now, and should also face prosecution for violating various federal conflict-of-interest standards. In any event, he seems also to be suffering from many of the same delusions plaguing President Bush, and is not a suitable replacement.

Little is now known about Laura Bush and her political capabilities. The same was true of Edith Wilson, who quietly took over for Woodrow after her husband drove himself to mental ruin during World War I and his campaign for the League of Nations. While touring Europe for his beloved world organization, Wilson was debilitated by a stroke. Rather than risk a constitutional crisis, Edith secretly assumed much of the day-to-day management of the presidency. Quietly but effectively, she kept the chaotic post-war White House on an even keel.

By contrast, Nancy Reagan was a very public figure. Her career as an actress had made her comfortable on the public stage. A master manipulator, she inspired both deep loyalty and lasting enmity. Most of the public assumed her politics were extremely conservative. But in fact she despised the fundamentalist right wing then moving toward control of the GOP, referring to them as "extra chromosome" Republicans.

As her husband's mental faculties began to fail, she looked for a family legacy. Firing White House chief of staff Donald Regan, it was Nancy who engineered Ronnie's triumphant agreements with the Soviet Union and Mikhail Gorbachev, bringing an end to the Cold War. Sources as diverse as gossip writer Kitty Kelly and leftist stalwart Barbara Ehrenreich argue that the real architect of the new peace was the wife of the President.

Could we expect such great things from Laura Bush? We don't know. She has been among the most silent and non-intrusive of First Ladies. Her only recent foray into the public eye involved her attempt to convene a conference of poets. It was promptly cancelled when it became clear many of them would speak against her husband's war.

But her husband now seems in a mental state similar to those that forced the phase-out of Presidents Wilson and Reagan. We urge readers to write to Laura Bush and ask that she assume leadership since the clock is running and innocent civilians in Baghdad are hours away from being slaughtered.

Here's our plea:

Dear Laura,

Having just witnessed the President's March 17 catatonic war declaration, although he did briefly show a flash of passion when he pleaded for the Iraqi people to save the oilfields, you must be just as worried about him as we are. While his cognitive impairments are well known, you have to be bothers by the recent rash of articles asking the singular question: "Is the President Nuts?"

We were shocked by the ease at which the President could explain why he was ignoring and bypassing the United Nations Security Council to teach Saddam Hussein a lesson for not cooperating with the same Security Council. Laura, you know more than anyone else that the President's recent actions and especially the March 17 speech are a desperate cry for help. We don't know what you had to do to sober him up after his two decades of admitted substance abuse. Whatever tough love you used, you must resort to it again. The President is not a well man.

Think of his legacy. Follow the examples set by Nancy Reagan and Edith Wilson. Drive, as Nancy used to like to say, "the extra-chromosome Republicans" from the White House. Put out strict orders that nobody from the American Enterprise Institute, who are most likely responsible for the President's drugged appearance, is to have any contact with him.

If you need any assistance, we stand ready for an old-fashioned intervention.

THE FUNDAMENTALIST NIGHTMARE

George W. Bush has attacked Iraq and put the world into a horrific vice that's the global peace movement's ultimate challenge: stopping a holy war that can only escalate into irrational mass slaughter. In traditional geopolitical terms, the downward spiral of this catastrophic American attack has been fairly straightforward. Among other things:

• For weeks the entire world was riveted on Bush's campaign to win nine of 15 votes on the Security Council to endorse the attack on Iraq. When he failed, he treated the UN as if it were no longer relevant, potentially weakening it for decades to come.

• UN weapons inspectors, led by Hans Blix, reported good progress in disarming Iraq right up to the moment the U.S. attacked. They reacted angrily when their work was cut short. By attacking Iraq after it at least partially disarmed, the U.S. may have doomed future UN disarmament efforts.

• In conjunction with those efforts, credible reports that Iraq rid itself of chemical and biological weapons as early as 1991 were published throughout the world, shredding Bush's argument that war was needed to destroy such weapons.

• Claims made by Secretary of State Colin Powell and other ranking Bush officials to the Congress, the UN and the world that Iraq was trying to buy large quantities of African uranium for the manufacture of nuclear weapons have been shown to be deliberate falsehoods, backed by crudely forged documents.

• When the campaign for a war to rid Iraq of Saddam's "weapons of mass destruction" failed to persuade, Bush switched to demanding a "regime change" that would mean "freedom" for the Iraqi people. But claims by Vice President Dick Cheney that Iraqis would greet invading Americans by "dancing in the streets," and other widely publicized promises of mass revolt by the Iraqi public, are now thoroughly discredited. As at Cuba's Bay of Pigs, in Vietnam and elsewhere throughout history, an invading military force expecting mass revolt has instead galvanized a nation around its own local leadership, no matter how brutal.

• Promises of minimum civilian casualties have been rendered tragically absurd by bombings of a Baghdad marketplace that killed or wounded at least a hundred innocents, and by other incidents in which Iraqi non-combatants have been slaughtered.

• War continues to rage in "pacified" Afghanistan, where the opium poppy crop has returned with a vengeance.

• China, India, Russia and Indonesia—four of the world's five largest nations, accounting for roughly half the planet's population—continue to express angry opposition to the attack, as does virtually all of Europe, Latin America and much of Africa.

• Domestic anti-war opinion within "allies" Spain and Italy is now in the 90-percent range, and is approaching that in Australia, where Prime Minister John Howard faces possible ouster from office.

• The Bush administration assumed it would routinely win permission to use long-time ally Turkey's land and air corridors. Despite a $26 billion bribe, permission was denied, mainly due to 90-percent Turkish opposition;

• Resignations within the administration indicate an increasingly isolated pro-war junta that may be divided within itself, as witnessed by the resignation of super-hawk Richard Perle, often dubbed "the prince of darkness," to pursue more lucrative options.

• Congressional moves toward impeaching Bush are escalating, accompanied by serious administration defeats on drilling for oil in Alaska and tax issues.

• Bush faces stiff resistance on funding for an extended occupation. His war budget may be a staggering $75 billion just for the first month. By contrast, his father's 1991 Gulf War cost the U.S. less than $5 billion.

• As war drags on, the U.S. economy continues to sink into chaos and despair, with the dollar plunging worldwide, losing its long-standing global dominance to the rapidly advancing euro.

Through it all, the worldwide anti-war movement—the SuperPower of Peace—has continued to grow and mature. Mass demonstrations in 300 or more cities around the planet continue to escalate in numbers and sophistication. Mid-sized cities regularly host three or more demonstrations running at the same time.

There have even been cracks in the mainstream media, whose corporate domination has rendered it almost unanimously pro-war. The hawkish *Washington Post* has taken to printing serious critiques of Bush's attack strategy. Normally servile reporters at military briefings have begun to ask difficult questions.

Extreme-right outlets such as Fox News and the Clear Channel radio network have escalated their attack on the peace movement, labeling it everything from frivolous to treasonous. But street demonstrations continue to expand and the level of organization is growing more sophisticated. Meanwhile financial and economic leaders worldwide are raising ever more pointed questions about the wisdom of this horrendous war and its long-term impact on economic stability within the U.S. and around the world.

Tied together by the Internet, with deepened commitments to non-violence, the SuperPower of Peace may indeed have achieved unprecedented global strength.

But it must now come to grips with the realities of sectarian psychosis, starting with the White House. George W. Bush's initial characterization of his war posture as a "crusade" against "evil" may prove all too accurate—and its fundamentalist Christian roots are now almost certain to elicit a horrific response from fundamentalist Islam.

Bush has already made it clear he will not hesitate to use nuclear weapons wherever his whims might take him. Richard Nixon contemplated using them in Vietnam, but was deterred by the peace movement. But Bush's statements give clear indication that the people now running the United States may lack Nixon's political compass.

To be sure, the Internet is now chock full of thoughtful analyses about the role of global dominance, oil and the shrinking status of the dollar in motivating this attack. But it is abundantly clear that Bush believes he talks to his own very personal version of a Christian God, in this case a deity of death, dictatorship and the "end times" of Biblical prophecy as put forth in Ezekial, Isaiah and Revelations. Christian fundamentalist talk radio is brimming with the view that Bush is a prophet, sent to usher in Armageddon, starting in Babylon.

In short, this unelected but immensely powerful leader seems incapable of complex thought or introspection. He views the massive outpouring of millions of world citizens as something "irrelevant," to be cavalierly ignored in the face his own view of a higher purpose. If nothing else, Bush is blithely secure in the illusion that whatever he chooses to do, in war or otherwise, is divinely ordained.

Saddam's mere ouster can no longer fulfill the Bush agenda. While hugely lucrative contracts for "rebuilding" Iraq pour out to his super-rich cronies, it's become clear that no matter what the administration has in mind, a post-Saddam Middle East will—like the post-Shah Iran—swing wildly and irrevocably toward fundamentalist, anti-Western Islam, probably taking Pakistan and the rest of the Middle East with it.

This first week of war confirmed that Bush has already opened the fundamentalist Pandora's Box. Already there are unsurprising signs that Iran to the east and Syria to the west may be helping the Iraqis. In huge, nuke-armed Pakistan, once viewed as largely pro-Western, fundamentalist fervor is sweeping the grassroots.

In the wake of September 11, and now with Bush's clumsy, brutal attack on Iraq, the world is being crushed between the twin psychoses of the angry fundamentalist Islam of Osama bin Laden and the smug, self-righteous fundamentalist Christian views of the isolated, nuclear-armed Bush administration.

The SuperPower of Peace is gaining strength, sophistication and global reach. It may well be capable of meeting the traditional political realities of a war for oil and imperial domination. But it must now also anticipate the growing specter of a horrific jihad/crusade without end, a whole new level of theological psychosis and global disarray.

BLESSED
ARE THE
WARMONGERS

As our predominantly Christian nation prepared for the sacraments of Easter this spring, it was a good time to reflect on the unholy perils of the Bush administration's imperialist occupation of Iraq. The *New York Times* finally reported what the alternative press has been pointing out for nearly a year, that the U.S. is planning a long-term military occupation of Iraq, with the Pentagon is demanding long-term access to four key military bases there.

Alas, the shroud of Iraqi liberation is ripped away and the resurrected body of the new Roman Empire exposed. As the *Times* explained, "A military foothold in Iraq would be felt across the border in Syria, and in combination with the continued United States presence in Afghanistan it would virtually surround Iran with a new web of American influence."

Occupying the Middle East through bomber diplomacy, however, will be much more difficult than during the heyday of early 20th century U.S. gunboat diplomacy in Central America. The U.S. government has spent an estimate $50 billion a year since the last Gulf War establishing unwanted military bases in Saudi Arabia and now Qatar.

In fact, the reason the U.S.'s former ally Osama bin Laden turned against us in 1991 was over the U.S. military base in Saudi Arabia.

So, as 43 million Americans go without healthcare, our infrastructure rots and our public schools crumble, the federal government with its record $400 billion yearly budget deficit will again search for the Holy Grail in the sands of the Middle East: a Western military empire dominating the region's oil supply.

Where will it end?

The BBC reported Easter weekend that many in Syria believe that "There will be American tanks rumbling through the narrow streets" of Damascus next year. Syria's great sin: conflict with Israel. Syria backed Iran during the Iran-Iraq War, invaded Iraq with U.S.-led coalition troops in 1991, and aided the U.S. in its war against Al Qaeda. Still, the new American Empire rattles its sabers and demands obedience to the new sick Caesar.

Render unto Bush the Middle East, proclaims Cheney, Rumsfeld, Wolfowitz and Perle. And the majority of the American people say "Blessed are the warmongers, for they shall be called the Children of the U.K."

In the repressive heat of the Baghdad summer, the people go without water, electricity and sanitation services. The *Independent* of Britain reports that, "Baghdad, whose public services were once a First World standard, has slipped back 100 years."

The phones haven't worked since the liberating Americans bombed the exchange centers. Looted hospitals report new epidemics of water-borne diseases like dysentery, cholera, typhoid and polio, which have killed the majority of an estimated million Iraqis since sanctions were implemented following the Gulf War.

The *Independent* also notes that "recently declassified documents of the American Defense Intelligence Agency show the allies deliberately targeted Iraq water supply during the previous conflict—a war crime, not that most Americans care, as they busy themselves worshipping their version of an imperialist Christ who in reality was crucified in lands occupied by the Roman Empire."

Meanwhile, tens of thousands of Iraqis took to the streets on Good Friday demanding that American invaders cease the occupation of their country and leave their oil alone. The Saudi foreign minister, Prince Saud Al-Faisal, insisted to all who would listen that the U.S.-led forces have no legitimate right as occupiers to exploit Iraqi oil and that UN sanctions should remain in place until the Iraqi people establish their own legitimate government.

Reuters reported that U.S. officials insist that the Iraqi people will not be allowed to take possession of their oil wells and the revenues from them until their debt, estimated at more than $100 billion including war reparations, is paid off.

No wonder U.S. troops stood by while organized criminals looted the treasured antiquities of the world's oldest civilization, but the Oil Ministry was zealously protected by the Marines. The corps' hymn may now add, "From the halls of Montezuma to the shores of the Euphrates, we have fought our bankers' battles, on the air, on land and seas."

As U.S. Christians reflected on Jesus' time in the tomb on Saturday, the *Times of London* pondered the epidemic of U.S. cluster bomb injuries resulting from U.S. air attacks. On the day Jesus was crucified, three Iraqi boys between the ages of seven and 14 were killed and two others injured in cluster bomb explosions.

As American children hunted eggs on Sunday, Iraqi parents hunted for unexploded U.S.-made cluster bombs to protect their children.

Sergeant Jason Daniels told the *Times*, "They are a huge pain in the ass. The only way to get rid of them is to explode them one by one. What I heard is that they began using the cluster bombs because they ran out of high explosives."

I doubt that the American people will check the shrapnel-scarred face of Ali Hassan and realize that he resembles Christ, or that the injured legs of his brother Hala remind them of the tortured limbs of the Messiah. Their agony is transferred by imperial decree by the new Caesar into acceptable "collateral damage" as a result of "sorties" needed to "liberate" Iraq. And the vast majority of the American people said, "Amen."

BUSH'S
MILITARY
DEFEAT

George W. Bush has fittingly stopped short of declaring victory in Iraq. He doesn't want to claim a definitive triumph because it would legally obligate the U.S. to begin cleaning the place up and enforcing human rights obligations.

But in fact, the U.S. attacks on Iraq and Afghanistan have been shattering defeats. Let's count the ways:

• At least three times U.S. troops have fired live ammunition against angry crowds of "liberated" Iraqis. Far from "dancing in the streets" over the American presence, the people of Iraq have made it clear they want the U.S. out just days after the removal of Saddam Hussein, who most Iraqis understand was put in power by the U.S. in the first place.

• U.S. troops have now killed at least 20 Iraqis in demonstrations that appear to be nonviolent. Military claims of self-defense are reminiscent of lies that Kent State University students fired weapons during the May 1970 massacre there. Those four deaths put the U.S. in an uproar; in Iraq, less than one-tenth the size of the U.S., the equivalent of 20 dead would be more than 200.

• By independent count at least 3,000 Iraqi civilians were killed by the U.S. in the removal of Saddam. That would equate to more than 30,000 Americans if the attack had been by Iraq on the U.S.

• Like Osama bin Laden, Saddam Hussein is widely believed to be alive, but has yet to be found.

• The weapons of mass destruction used as a pretext for the American attack have also yet to be found. None were used in Iraq's defense.

• The pillaging of Iraq's most treasured museums, for which the U.S. is directly responsible, has been widely ranked as one of the most barbaric and indefensible acts of cultural desecration in world history.

• U.S. corporate media coverage of the Bush attack was so absurdly one-sided and nationalistic it drew unprecedented contempt from critics worldwide.

• The "victory" which has so enamored the U.S. corporate media was an assault by a rich nation of 280 million people—which spends more on its military than the rest of the world combined—against an impoverished, disunited nation that has been ruled by a hated dictator installed by the U.S., subjected to international sanctions for 12 years, continually bombed through that time, and which was recently disarmed by United Nations weapons inspectors. Far from a military triumph, Bush's martial performance drew mocking derision from the global media outside the U.S.

• The first female U.S. soldier killed in Iraq was Lori Ann Piestewa, a divorced Hopi-Navajo mother of two small children who joined the military to escape poverty. Her death, and the grim future facing her children, received virtually no media attention, while the dubious "rescue" of her white friend, Jessica Lynch, received ecstatic—and wildly distorted—hype.

• Defense Secretary Rumsfeld openly and willfully violated explicit U.S. law by failing to establish a baseline health study of American troops entering combat, reinforcing the failure to deal with Gulf War Syndrome from the previous attack on Iraq.

• Though fewer than a thousand U.S. troops were killed or wounded in the 1991 Gulf War, by some counts as many as 220,000 may be disabled. Similar casualties are almost certain to surface in the wake of the latest attack, though Rumsfeld's illegal refusal to lay the statistical groundwork for a health study will again make these ailments and their causes hard to track.

• It is widely believed Bush launched a lethal attack on the Palestine Hotel in Baghdad with the express intent of killing and intimidating foreign journalists.

• While profoundly disinterested in protecting the region's cultural history, or its civil institutions, the U.S. military took great pains to guard Saddam's ministries of interior and oil, where crucial information on Iraq's petroleum reserves are stored.

• U.S. military encampments during the attack were named after major oil companies.

• No major nations of the world except Great Britain joined the attack on Iraq, and none have come forward since to endorse it, despite Bush's alleged "victory." Though leading Bush administration hawks have raised the possibility of attacking Syria, Iran or North Korea, all other major nations of the world—including Great Britain—have denounced the possibility.

• Bush has scorned his previous promise to Great Britain's Tony Blair, his one major ally, that the rebuilding of Iraq would be largely done through the United Nations.

• Afghanistan has sunk into tribal warfare, complete with the rebirth of the "defeated" Taliban. American soldiers are still fighting and dying there.

• Despite Bush's effusive pre-war promises, there is virtually no money in the latest U.S. budget for rebuilding Afghanistan, or even for repairing the damage done by the U.S. attack. Drug production, particular opium poppies, is back in full swing in Afghanistan after having been successfully repressed by the Taliban.

• Bush's violent assault and undiplomatic arrogance have infuriated much of the Muslim world and made it highly likely fundamentalist, Iran-style regimes will eventually sweep over both Afghanistan and Iraq. That likelihood has been enhanced by anti-Islam statements from close Bush cronies, including Reverend Franklin Graham, who've confirmed Bush's initial proclamation of a "crusade."

• While crowing over bringing a new "democracy" to Iraq, Defense Secretary Rumsfeld says he will not "allow" fundamentalists to take power there, but has not explained how he would stop it within a democratic framework.

• By infuriating the Muslim world and isolating the U.S., Bush's conquests of Iraq and Afghanistan will likely guarantee a horrific increase in terrorist attacks in years to come. Polls show a large portion of the American public fears precisely this outcome.

In short, the Bush "triumph" has the taste and smell of a profound defeat. The Iraqi people have made it clear they want the U.S. out, and that the demonstrations can only escalate. Afghanistan is in ruin and chaos.

World opinion, so profoundly sympathetic to the U.S. after the horrors of September 11, has swung wildly against us. To the vast bulk of humanity—especially 1.2 billion Muslims—the U.S. is an out-of-control bully that invaded Iraq without legitimate provocation, primarily to grab its oil.

Only the grotesquely unbalanced and intolerant U.S. corporate media has supported this attack with any consistency. Worldwide, its credibility has sunk below zero.

The United States may be the only military superpower. But it's a hollow shell, with its domestic economy in profound crisis and the dollar in fast decline. The cynicism, arrogance and brutality with which Bush has carried out these attacks has provoked a profound, deep-rooted worldwide hostility.

Far from victory, the U.S. has never been more weakened, isolated or insecure. In the long run, only one superpower—the one for peace—holds any hope for any of us.

AYATOLLAH ROBERTSON'S SUPREME FATWAH

Ayatollah Pat Robertson is praying for the departure of at least three Justices of the United States Supreme Court. And the Bush junta continues its relentless attack on the foundations of American democracy. The "shock and awe" of this ever-escalating blitzkreig has been the root of Bush's strength, keeping the opposition off balance and on the defensive.

But cracks are showing in a totalitarian assault that needs total victory. The regime has grossly overreached its minority non-mandate. Its procession of big lies, such as Saddam's nonexistent weapons of mass destruction, are generating just the kind of blowback that can shatter a tyranny, even one in control of the mass media.

Have we turned a corner?

Robertson's "prayer" for the "removal" of three Supreme Court Justices reeks of a "fatwah"—a call to murder. Islamic ayatollahs issued a similar death threat against Salman Rushdie, whose *Satanic Verses* they deemed blasphemous. In fact, he merely lampooned the ayatollahs. Against all odds, Rushdie still lives.

Robertson has condemned the Supreme Court for supporting a woman's right to choose and for guaranteeing the right of citizens to make love in ways Robertson doesn't like. Appointed for life, the Supremes can retire or die. So if one of his followers kills them, who will Robertson thank first? God?

Robertson and his fellow ayatollahs, Franklin Graham and Jerry Falwell, hate more than just gays: they hate America, specifically the Bill of Rights, the Constitution, diversity of opinion and ethnicity, freedom of worship, the idea that all people are created equal.

Their messiah, George W. Bush, is under fire for running the most secretive, dishonest and repressive administration in U.S. history.

With his signature lack of integrity, Bush blames anyone and everyone for his recent whopper about Saddam Hussein's nukes. He stuck a knife in Tony Blair's back. He trashed the CIA. He fingered an obscure White House functionary. Along the way he illegally outed a covert agent, the wife of Ambassador Joseph Wilson, the highly respected researcher who long ago told Bush that Saddam had no nukes. When investigative reporter Sy Hersh originally broke this story, the administration used the word "terrorist" to describe him.

Meanwhile, Bush has skulked away from the September 11 inquest. Cheney's energy policy and Bush's stock frauds remain shrouded in state secrecy. This is a supremely cynical gang of thieves, addicted to secrecy, happy to stab anyone, any time.

Along with a crashing economy, Bush's polls are in a tail spin. But his strategy remains the same: attack, attack, attack. Every phrase of the Constitution, every guarantee in the Bill of Rights, every icon of social welfare, every shred of environmental protection, no matter how eminently sane or universally accepted, is under relentless assault. For example:

• In Head Start, the junta assaulted a much-loved program that has helped millions of American children for decades.

• In attacking the global treaty on the ozone layer, Bush is pushing methyl bromide, a marginal pesticide, one of the last chemicals in use that does serious ozone damage. Global consensus for this treaty is even more solid than on global warming; experts everywhere are stunned.

• In indicting Greenpeace USA for a peaceful action against rainforest mahogany in Miami harbor last year, the junta has served notice it will aggressively prosecute non-violent civil protests.

• The junta used Homeland Security forces to hunt down Texas Democrats resisting an outrageous redistricting ordered by GOP hitman Tom DeLay. Congressional districts are traditionally redesigned every 10 years. But with a new majority in the state legislature, the GOP is demanding a coup.

• Congressional Republicans called out the Capitol police against Democrats who dared try to caucus outside a committee hearing.

• Bush's horrific ultra-right judicial appointments have outraged even moderate Democrats, prompting the GOP leadership to contemplate trashing traditional Senatorial safeguards they used against Bill Clinton.

• California's first-ever gubernatorial recall will cost taxpayers $30 million. Bought by a Republican extremist millionaire with virtually no grassroots support, the recall is aimed at the Democratic Party in its strongest state— and at the state itself.

• ESPN has given Rush Limbaugh a platform to turn professional football into a Republican bullhorn. Limbaugh's infamous racism will apply to many of the players whose performances he'll describe.

• Major media continue to present no-talent hate mongers like Ann Coulter and Charles Krauthammer as if they were serious reporters or scholars, when their sole claim to air time is one-note contempt for anything green or humanist.

But despite its total grip on the government and media, the junta's popularity sags. It plunged into a desert quagmire with no exit strategy for one obvious reason: Iraqi oil is the Bush Energy Plan. With the economy in free fall, Bush must drive down gas prices for the 2004 election. So U.S. troops will spill every last drop of their blood to secure every last drop of that oil.

The Bush strategy is to hog-tie its critics over every inch of turf, no matter how safe it once seemed. Given the horrors of the U.S. concentration camp at Guantanamo, it seems all too clear the junta is capable of using the Patriot Act and Homeland Security apparatus for Soviet-style arrests and Latin-style disappearances even of moderate critics and internal opponents.

Yet America's pro-democracy movement has exploded at the grassroots, through the Internet and over the few talk radio outlets remaining open to diversity.

Tom Paine described an earlier crisis in American democracy as a time to try our souls. Today yet another aggressive and intolerant tyranny has decided to up the ante. Will we have the strength and wisdom to win again?

FITRAKIS
August 1, 2003

THE COVER-UP IS THE CRIME

While the mainstream media debates whether the President was misinforming, exaggerating or misleading the U.S. public, they miss the bigger story—their obvious complicity with the Bush administration's Nazi-style propaganda prior to the war.

George W. Bush and his administration deliberately undertook a massive campaign to wage illegal and aggressive war against the people of Iraq. The narrow focus on one fraudulent claim in the State of the Union address regarding Iraq buying uranium from Africa ignores the much broader campaign of falsification used to whip the people into a war frenzy.

Take the second obvious lie: that Iraq was harboring and supporting Al Qaeda terrorists. The mainstream media knew that Saddam Hussein and Osama bin Laden were arch-enemies and represented two distinct ideological movements, Hussein's pan-Arab movement and bin Laden's fundamentalist pan-Islamic movement. The only thing these two men had in common was that both had been decade-long U.S. allies in the 1980s. Which country is most responsible for harboring Al Qaeda? We know the answer. The United States of America, where they learned to fly and where they attacked on September 11 after the Bush administration called the FBI off their trail.

Bush and his cabinet, enabled by the media, tell blatant and verifiable lies daily. Take for example Bush's latest fabrication on July 15, 2003. During a news briefing with UN Secretary General Kofi Annan, the President stated, "The larger point is, and the fundamental question is, did Saddam Hussein have a weapons program? And the answer is, absolutely. And we gave him a chance to let the inspectors in, and he wouldn't let them in. And, therefore, after a reasonable request, we decided to remove him from power, along with other nations."

The fact that Bush would so drastically alter reality, with the world's leading advocate of weapons inspections beside him, and the images of UN weapons inspectors night after night on U.S. TV news, suggests that the President is either mentally unstable or a pathological liar far worse than Richard Nixon.

Moreover, the UN Security Council specifically refused to sanction the U.S.-British attack on Iraq. It was only an imminent attack that forced out the weapons inspectors.

The more important question may not be the sanity of the President but why the mainstream media allows Dubya to openly, notoriously and outrageously lie. Do presidential lies matter only if they involve oral sex with an intern? Are they perfectly acceptable if done in the style of the Third Reich to support the return of a 19th century imperialist occupation of a Third World people?

Perhaps the U.S. press embraces the silence of the lamb because, as the book *Into the Buzzsaw* notes, our best investigative reporters are routinely fired, laid off, demoted or silenced when they challenge corruption in high places. Or, are the media simply afraid that sinister forces in our own military-industrial complex will send them grade-A, made-in-the-USA anthrax to intimidate them?

The unaltered fact remains that the only reason Dubya is President today is because his brother, Governor Jeb Bush of Florida, ordered election supervisors to purge some 58,000 voters from the Florida rolls—not because they were felons, but because their names were the same or similar to felons. This news story surfaced on the front page—in Britain.

Rather than really thinking of the media as being lazy or indifferent, we should see that Bush's illegal war campaign exposes them as willing accomplices. As media critic Robert McChesney points out, "[There has been a] striking consolidation of the media from hundreds of firms to an industry dominated by 10 enormous transnational conglomerates. The largest 10 media firms own all U.S. TV networks, most TV stations, all major film studios, all major music companies, nearly all cable TV channels, much of the book and magazine publishing, and much, much more."

And we have the Secretary of State's son, Michael Powell, at the FCC advocating more media consolidation, yelling like Bush, "Bring it on!"

Is it any wonder that the public is entranced with so-called "reality TV" while our military produces fictional stories like the "Saving of Private Lynch?" The military scripts neo-American hokum and does Hollywood at its finest, the feel-good tale of the American girl-next-door in the middle of a firefight with evil Iraqi men trying to kill her until her last ammunition clip was emptied. When the Iraqi medical staff tried to return her to the U.S. troops, after she was injured solely by a vehicle crash, they were met with gunfire to keep them at the hospital until the military video crew could arrive and tape the blockbuster fantasy for the nightly news.

Still, the biggest lie that Bush has perpetrated on the U.S. public that has escaped any and all scrutiny is the blatant illegality of the war. There is no such thing as "preventive war" under international law or UN Charter. No nation has the right to change the "regime" of another nation because they don't like their leaders; nor can a nation attack another because they may pose a threat years in the future. Bizarrely, the U.S. mainstream media allows the President to routinely violate international law unchallenged.

So it is not surprising the Bush administration uses Nazi-style propaganda to resurrect long-discredited doctrines like preventive war. The Fourth Reich will come to the U.S. in the name of fighting terrorism and protecting "homeland security."

BUSH TO NEW YORKERS: DROP DEAD

George W. Bush has officially told the people of New York City that as far as he's concerned, they can drop dead. And thanks to his lies, many of them will. With his latest attack on the Clean Air Act he's said the same to millions more.

Bush has used the September 11 "trifecta" to build his popularity, fund the military and tear up the Bill of Rights. But the GOP's cynical uses of the tragedy have reached a new level.

The White House directly interfered with planned Environmental Protection Agency warnings about the toxic fallout from the World Trade Center explosions. It had "competing considerations" that came before protecting the health of the people of New York. Among them were reopening the stock exchange as quickly as possible, and limiting clean-up costs and liability claims.

Because of Bush's lies, thousands of Americans will suffer cancers, emphysema, heart attack, stroke, birth defects, stillbirths, sterility, eye/ear/nose/throat disease and much more.

There have been few toxic events to match the explosions that pulverized the two World Trade Center towers. The short-term deaths of 3,000 people will be dwarfed over the long term by the lethal fallout.

These were two of the last big buildings constructed with asbestos, whose health effects are infamous. Once ingested, the fibers can and do make cells cancerous. Thousands of miners and others exposed to asbestos have filed lawsuits against Johns-Manville and others.

The EPA knew that spewing all that asbestos into New York's air was a horrific event, and that lives could be saved by taking certain public precautions. Bush stopped that from happening.

The World Trade Center also contained countless computer screens, light fixtures, calculators, telephones, network servers, paging systems, copy machines and much more high-tech office equipment laden with mercury and other toxic metals. The concrete, flooring, plastics, chemical cleaners, furniture, metal struts, window glass—all that was also pulverized into a horrific brew of murderous dioxins, furans and lethal powders with hideous killing power.

Where did it all come down? Who has breathed it? How many were elderly? Who might be uniquely sensitive? How many were pregnant, with vulnerable embryos?

How far did their lethal powder spread through the region? Where is it now? How long will those poisons kill again and again and yet again? What could be done to prevent further sickness and death?

As the EPA knew, those living nearby were owed detailed information—which was denied them by Bush. So were those working in the ruins for days, weeks and months. And those who have innocently proceeded with lives downwind.

At very least, people working on or near the site should have been wearing respirators. All downwind buildings should have been intensely monitored. Many should have been fitted with advanced filtration units. All carpeting, furniture, walls and fixtures should have been repeatedly measured and cleaned. And then cleaned again. And then cleaned yet again.

But such things cost money. And some buildings might never have reopened. And the stock market might have stayed shut longer. Lives would have been saved, but Bush decided they were less valuable than those competing considerations.

Now he's decimated the Clean Air Act, allowing more power plant emissions in yet another giveaway to the rich corporations that fund the GOP. So more Americans will die. But Bush will have more money to spend on his 2004 re-election campaign.

This man has horribly wronged the people of New York, whose terrible tragedies he continues to exploit. He puts us all at risk in exchange for campaign contributions.

New Yorkers—all Americans—suffer and die as a result. It's a debt that can never be repaid.

AMERICA'S DEMONSTRATION DEMOCRACY

During the Cold War, the CIA, in the words of long-time agent Ralph McGehee, practiced the art of "deadly deceits." Throughout the Third World, the secret spy agency engaged in covert operations, blatant acts of economic destabilization and wanton acts of mass violence.

In the 1970s, Idaho Senator Frank Church's investigatory committee established that the CIA also engaged in so-called "benign" operations, including rigging elections. The agency used the term "demonstration elections"—elections that are superficially democratic but with results manipulated by the CIA.

Central Intelligence Agency did everything from stuffing ballot boxes, creating political parties, merging smaller political parties into large coalitions (as in Uno in Nicaragua), paying death squads to intimidate voters, and the occasional use of computer fraud.

In the mid-1980s, the Reagan administration used a computer to help their "man in Panama" and CIA asset Manuel Noriega gain electoral support. They backed dictator Ferdinand Marcos when he brought in pre-programmed voting-machine tapes in the middle of an election to turn his sure defeat into a fixed victory. The people of the Philippines didn't accept the computer results as credible, but President Reagan and Vice President Bush (himself a former CIA director) argued it was necessary to preserve our "traditional" relationship with the brutal dictator. Remember, his political opponent, Senator Aquino, was shot to death after disembarking from an airplane to run against Marcos.

Now that we have the son of the former CIA director as President, we should recognize that the more reprehensible tactics of the CIA have been brought home with the Bush dynasty. What George W. Bush's energy friends from Texas, including Enron, did to the California economy through the massive "mega-watt" laundering of electricity should be viewed as just another destabilization of an enemy regime.

The 2000 Florida election included all of the signs of a Third World CIA demonstration election: bizarrely constructed butterfly ballots, obscure third parties receiving unexplained and unfathomable votes, and heavily Jewish areas voting unexpectedly for right-wing anti-Semitic candidates like Pat Buchanan. Remember that the exit polls predicted that Gore would win. Only when the psych-ops operation at Fox News changed that call did some people begin to believe in the myth of the Bush victory.

What began as covert operations in the Third World are now overt practices by the Bush administration in the United States.

Take for example the August 14, 2003, letter from Walden O'Dell, chief executive of Diebold Inc., pledging that he is "committed to helping Ohio deliver its votes to the President next year."

Diebold is one of three finalists currently seeking the $100 million contract with the state of Ohio to provide computerized voting machines for the 2004 elections. Diebold has worked on its computers with Battelle, a well-established collaborator with the U.S. military and CIA. (Battelle was also the contractor for Voter News Service and failed to produce exit polls for the 2002 Congressional election.)

Computer scientists from John Hopkins have indicated that it would be relatively easy to hack into and manipulate the computer voting results in these machines. Detailed analyses of the flaws in Diebold's electronic voting machines can be easily found on the Internet.

The *Seattle Times* ran a feature story on Diebold in its August 21 edition. Bev Harris, a Seattle-area public relations company owner, recently uncovered "some 4,000 files that included user manuals, source code and executable files for voting machines made by Diebold, a corporation based in North Canton, Ohio."

So what do we have here, other than the obvious denial by mainstream America? We've got a CIA family and their corporate supporters working with CIA contractors at Battelle in order to bring flawed electronic voting to the U.S.—machines that leave in their wake no paper trails and questionable exit polls.

Factor in the reality that, out of 435 Congressional districts in the U.S., only 39, or nine percent, are actually competitive (where major party candidates won with less than 55 percent of the vote). Under our political system, the vast majority of Congressional seats are gerrymandered as "safe," or noncompetitive, by the party that controls the state government. Eleven Texas Democrats are hiding out in New Mexico in hopes of thwarting another round of Republican district-rigging in their state. So little democracy is actually left.

Over the years, well-known and respected political theorists and leaders have warned of the rise of authoritarianism. In the 1950s, President Eisenhower warned of the "military-industrial complex." C. Wright Mills detailed the "power elite"—the convergence of the top levels of the military, corporations and governmental leaders during the Cold War.

In the 1960s, Herbert Marcuse, who worked for the Office of Strategic Services during World War II, pointed out that Americans' inability to think critically was making us a "one-dimensional" society with an authoritarian culture. In the 1970s, political scientists like William Domhoff and Thomas Dye began to document empirically the undemocratic and elitist nature of the U.S. political system.

In the 1980s, Bertrand Gross warned of the rise of "friendly fascism." In the 1990s, William Grieder documented that the U.S. had the best democracy money can buy and asked the question, "Who will tell the people?"

But the most damning and lasting testimony that foretold the rise of America's authoritarian "democracy" are the massive volumes produced by the Church Committee. Back in the late 1970s, the CIA's shadowy hands were all over the Idaho ABC Committee (Anybody But Church), which produced the defeat of the courageous senator.

Bush's election coup of 2000, the first overt CIA-style demonstration election in the U.S., gave the Bush clan and their allies in the intelligence community the opportunity to field test whether you can blatantly steal an American election just like in Panama or the Philippines. The

September 11 attacks provided Dubya with the authority to push U.S. society massively to the right and pursue militarism and imperialism. It also allowed Bush to test market neo-Nazi-style mass propaganda to the American public.

The voting machines are simply the final nail in the people's coffin. The comatose electorate rests silently as the hammer of authoritarianism falls.

WASSERMAN
September 24, 2003

ARNOLD STALKS FOR BUSH 2004

Anyone who thinks that the White House and Karl Rove are not behind the Arnold Schwarzenegger assault is not paying attention. A Schwarzenegger victory in California could ensure another White House win for George W. Bush.

The Republican juggernaut now controls the governorships of New York, Texas and Florida. With California they'd own the Statehouses of America's four biggest states—plus the White House, Congress, the judiciary and the media. Is there another word for one-party rule?

In 2000, Governor Jeb Bush guaranteed his brother's grab of the White House. There were many twists and turns, but the core of the coup came with the systematic removal of more than 50,000 "convicted felons"—people of color and other suspected Democrats—from Florida's voting lists. Computer voting machine manipulations may have cost Al Gore thousands more votes with a few keystrokes. But ultimately, it was Jeb's control of the Florida Statehouse that gave his brother the White House.

In Texas, Governor Rick "Goodhair" Perry is now strong-arming the legislature to give Republicans a deeper hold on the U.S. House of Representatives. Redistricting normally occurs every 10 years. But when the GOP took the Texas legislature in 2002, Perry began calling special sessions to ram through a redistricting plan that would all but eliminate Democrats from the Lone Star congressional delegation.

House Democrats first foiled that plan by fleeing to Oklahoma. U.S. House Majority Leader Tom DeLay sent Homeland Security after them, drawing widespread hoots from those who believe we still have a Bill of Rights in this country.

Then Senate Democrats derailed Perry's second special session by fleeing to Arizona, though one of them finally defected. Despite widespread outcry, Perry has called a third special session, at an overall cost of more than $1.5 million to angry Texas taxpayers.

Now Schwarzenegger is set to extend the GOP's control to California.

Governor Gray Davis did open the door by groveling at the feet of Southern California Edison and other utilities that gouged the state during the 2000-2001 electric deregulation fiasco. But that disaster's prime mover was none other than Schwarzenegger's chief advisor, Pete Wilson. As Governor, Wilson rammed the dereg bill through the legislature in 1996.

Written by Southern California Edison, the infamous AB1890 handed some $30 billion in ratepayer and taxpayer charges to private utilities. It then opened the door to Enron, Reliant and other GOP gas dealers, who grabbed another $60 billion. Among the beneficiaries was Kenneth "Kenny-Boy" Lay, George W. Bush's number one campaign contributor.

Despite all that, California's financial crisis is actually about average for the Age of Bush, in which virtually all the states are on the brink of bankruptcy.

Schwarzenegger is a clown candidate whose ignorance of the issues hides beneath the smokescreen of his bizarre celebrity. At the end of a dying film career, the Terminator's boorish sexism masks his foot soldier role in a totalitarian tragedy.

Make no mistake about it: Arnold is being spammed straight from the White House. He's there to purge those voter rolls, sabotage the state legislature, and do to California what's been done to Florida and Texas—and the nation.

Hasta la vista, American democracy.

SIEGE HEIL: THE NAZI NEXUS

Geeorge W. Bush's grandfather helped finance the Nazi Party. Arnold Schwarzenegger's Austrian father volunteered for the infamous Nazi SA and became a ranking officer. And Karl Rove can't hide his joy at witnessing "a Nazi rally" in support of Bush.

Together, they have destabilized California and are on the brink of bringing it a new Reich. With the Schwarzenegger candidacy they have laid siege to America's largest state, lining it up for the 2004 presidential election.

The Bush family's ties to the Nazi party are well known. In their 1994 book *Secret War Against the Jews*, Mark Aarons and John Loftus use official U.S. documents to establish that George Herbert Walker, George W. Bush's great-grandfather, was one of Hitler's most important early backers. He funneled money to the rising young fascist through the Union Banking Corporation.

In 1926, Walker arranged to have his new son-in-law, Prescott Bush—father of President George Herbert Walker Bush, grandfather of President George Walker Bush—hired as vice president at W.A. Harriman and Company. Prescott became a senior partner when Harriman merged with a British-American investment company to become Brown Brothers

Harriman. In 1934 Prescott Bush joined the board of directors of Union Banking.

The bank helped Hitler rise to power. It also helped him wage war. As late as July 31, 1941—well after the Nazi invasion of Poland—the U.S. government froze $3 million in Union Banking assets linked to Fritz Thyssen. Thyssen was noted in the American press as a "German industrialist and original backer of Adolph Hitler."

Loftus writes that Thyssen's "American friends in New York City...[were] Prescott Bush and Herbert Walker, the father and father-in-law of a future President of the United States." That would be the current president's father, former President George Herbert Walker Bush, also the former CIA director.

On October 20, 1942, the U.S. government ordered the seizure of Nazi Germany's banking operations in New York City, which were under the direction of Prescott Bush. The government seized control of Union Banking Corporation under the Trading with the Enemy Act. The liquidation yielded a reported $750,000 apiece for Prescott Bush and George Herbert Walker.

Loftus documents that "Prescott Bush knowingly served as a money launderer for the Nazis. Remember that Union Bank's books and accounts were frozen by the U.S. Alien Property Custodian in 1942 and not released back to the Bush family until 1951."

The book *The Splendid Blonde Beast: Money, Law and Genocide* also goes into exhaustive detail on the Bush-Harriman Nazi money laundering. More recently, Michael Kranish covers the same Bush-Nazi relationships in *The Rise of the Bush Family Dynasty*, published in the *Boston Globe*.

Often ignored are the Bush family's post-World War II dealings with former Nazis. John Foster Dulles, who had worked with the Bush family in the Harriman Company in laundering money for Nazi Germany, was Dwight Eisenhower's Secretary of State. His brother Allen became CIA director.

As Martin Lee documents in *The Beast Reawakens*, American intelligence recruited numerous top Nazis to spy on the Soviets during the Cold War. Many established connections to the Bush family that had helped finance their original rise to power.

In 1988, in its top annual award, Project Censored noted that "the major mass media ignored, overlooked or undercovered at least 10 critical stories reported in America's alternative press that raised serious questions about the Republican candidate, George Bush, dating from his reported role as a CIA 'asset' in 1963 to his presidential campaign's connection with a network of anti-Semites with Nazi and fascist affiliations in 1988." Investigative reporter Russ Bellant established ties between the Republican Party and former Axis Nazis and fascists.

In 2000 and 2001, the weekly newspaper *Columbus Alive* published a series of articles documenting further links between the elder President Bush and the Reverend Sun Myung Moon and his own fascist networks in Japan and Korea.

This sort of shadowy intrigue with authoritarian and anti-democratic networks suits Karl Rove, who serves as "Bush's Brain" in the current White House and is the political mastermind behind the California coup.

Rove is now being accused of involvement in the outing of a CIA covert operative, the wife of Ambassador Joseph Wilson. A consummate strategist, Rove may have outed Wilson's wife in retaliation for Wilson's failure to back up the Bush claim that Saddam Hussein was buying nuclear weapons materials in Africa. According to some published reports, as many as 70 CIA operatives may have been put at risk by Rove's alleged retaliatory strike.

Rove, who has been based in Utah and associated with the Mormon Church, is widely viewed as the chief engineer of the current Bush administration. He and Tom DeLay are attempting to force the Texas legislature to redistrict its congressional delegations, adding seven sure seats to the Republican column. By controlling the Statehouses in New York, Florida, Texas and California, the GOP would have a lock on the four largest states in the union, and the ability to manipulate vote counts and strip voter registration rolls in the run-up to the 2004 election.

Rove is a prime behind-the-scenes mover in the Schwarzenegger campaign. On May 1, 1939, a year after the Nazis took control of Schwarzenegger's native Austria, his father Gustav voluntarily joined Hilter's infamous Strumabteilung (SA), "brown shirt" stormtroopers. This was just six months after the brown shirts played a key role in the bloody Kristallnacht attacks on Germany's Jewish community.

The Vienna daily *Der Standard* noted recently that "Gustav, a high-ranking Nazi, brought up the bespectacled, rather frail boy with an iron fist and quite a few slaps in the face." Arnold's father favored a Hitler-style mustache in photos.

On October 3, ABC News broke the story of Schwarzenegger's 1975 interview in which he was asked whom he admired. Schwarzenegger replied, "I admire Hitler, for instance, because he came from being a little man with almost no formal education, up to power. I admire him for being such a good public speaker and for what he did with it."

To cover himself, Schwarzenegger has made substantial donations to the Los Angeles-based Wiesenthal Center, which tracks down ex-Nazis. Schwarzenegger has also renounced Hitler.

But he has not renounced his friendship with fellow Austrian Kurt Waldheim, the one-time head of the United Nations with known Nazi ties. The book *Arnold: An Unauthorized Biography* documents Schwarzenegger toasting Waldheim, who had participated in Nazi atrocities during World War II, at his wedding to Maria Shriver.

"My friends don't want me to mention Kurt's name, because of all the recent Nazi stuff and the UN controversy," Schwarzenegger said. "But I love him and Maria does to, and so thank you, Kurt."

On May 17, 2001, Schwarzenegger also met with Kenneth "Kenny-Boy" Lay of Enron infamy at the Peninsula Hotel in Los Angeles. Through the utility deregulation plan signed into law by then-Governor Pete Wilson, now Schwarzenegger's chief advisor, California was destabilized, bankrupting the state government and opening the door for the recall election. Lay has been George W. Bush's chief financial backer, and a close associate of Karl Rove's.

According to Bob Woodward's *Bush at War*, Bush attended a New York Yankees game soon after the September 11 World Trade Center disaster. He wore a fireman's jacket. As he threw out the first pitch, the crowd roared. Thousands of fans stuck out their arms with thumbs up.

Karl Rove, sitting in the box of Yankee owner George Steinbrenner, likened the roar of the crowd to "a Nazi rally."

Apparently he would know.

THE BUSH-NAZI NEXUS GOES MAINSTREAM

Senator Robert Byrd, on the floor of Congress on October 17, explicitly compared the Bush media operation to that run by Hermann Goering, mastermind of the Nazi putsch against the German people.

On the same day, the Associated Press published a story linking Prescott Bush to Adolf Hitler. The lead read: "President Bush's grandfather was a director of a bank seized by the federal government because of its ties to a German industrialist who helped bankroll Adolf Hitler's rise to power, government documents show."

That night, CNN ran a "streamer" on the bottom of its news programming confirming that "declassified documents show Prescott Bush connections to Nazi finance."

Stories reminding the public that the grandfather of President George W. Bush and his United Trust Bank were cited by the U.S. government in 1942 for helping Hitler under the Trading With the Enemies Act have now spread widely through the major media.

What's going on here? Are these stories linking the Bush family to the Nazis irrelevant? Mere partisan politics? Or do they indicate a growing public concern with what is actually happening in Washington?

Coming on the floor of the U.S. Senate, Byrd's searing critique indicates that the equation of the Bush administration with the Nazi elite has gained a certain mainstream credibility. A conservative Democrat who has represented West Virginia in the Senate for decades, Byrd is one of America's leading Constitutional scholars. He is known as the master of Senate procedures. A passionate student of the English language, his epic orations for peace and the preservation of historic American freedoms are likely to grace school texts for decades to come.

That the cautious, thoughtful Byrd has conjured explicit comparisons between the infamous mass murderer Goering and the administration of George W. Bush is a stunning commentary on how far to the right the Republicans have really gone. Goering was convicted of crimes against humanity at the Nuremberg war crimes tribunal after World War II. He killed himself just before he was to be executed.

That the mainstream media has again found newsworthy the long-established connections between the Bush family and the Nazi Party is also instructive.

For 60 years it has been a matter of public record that Prescott Bush helped finance Hitler's rise to power and world war. Later a U.S. Senator from Connecticut, Prescott was father to President George H.W. Bush and grandfather to George W. Bush. Because legal action was taken, Bush's deeds were widely covered in newspapers and electronic media at the time. The history is readily accessible.

But right-wing Bush fanatics continue to deny those ties existed. In a nationally syndicated radio show, conservative talk host Michael Medved recently claimed that Prescott Bush's bank's ties to the Nazis had not been established.

Similar denials have surrounded Arnold Schwarzenegger. It is a matter of public record that his father volunteered for the Austrian Nazi Party and the infamous SA, which engaged in brutal mass murder. Arnold himself has attempted to distance himself from his family's Nazi past. He has made large donations to the Wiesenthal Center in Los Angeles, which has tracked Nazi fugitives. His backers now claim he attended an anti-Nazi rally at an early age.

On the other hand, he has been linked to statements admiring Hitler for his speaking ability and his ability to gain a huge following. A past indicating a strong authoritarian nature has also been cause for alarm. In 1975, Schwarzenegger yearned for his own Nazi-style rally, "like Hitler in the

Nuremberg stadium. And have all those people scream at you and just being [in] total agreement whatever you say."

Bush supporters deny his Nazi family ties have anything to do with Republican policies. Visiting the "sins of the father" (or grandfather) on an offspring has not been considered fair game in U.S. politics.

But after eight years of total assault on Bill Clinton and his family, one can only imagine the media frenzy had Clinton's grandparents been linked to the Soviet Union. Would Rush Limbaugh or Karl Rove have found such ties "irrelevant"?

Does Rush's apparent narcotic addiction resemble that of Hermann Goering? Is he the right's real minister of propaganda? Do his "Dittoheads" resemble the unthinking brownshirts that terrorized millions?

Such things can be hard to hear. In polite society, they can strain "credibility." But blood ties and shallow images were not what Senator Byrd's comparisons between Bush and Goering were about: They were about Bush's actual behavior.

Like Byrd, tens of millions of Americans are deeply worried that this administration has waged an unprecedented assault on American civil rights and liberties. It has shredded the Constitution and the natural environment as none other in U.S. history. Its unprovoked attacks on Afghanistan and Iraq have prompted thoughtful comparisons to the unprovoked Nazi invasion of Poland in 1939. Its illegal detainment center at Guantanamo and its cavalier use of the drug war, the prison system and the powers arrogated through the Patriot Act and the Homeland Security apparatus have brought the U.S. to the brink of dictatorship.

Given the horrific reality of what the GOP is now doing to America and the world, we should be profoundly thankful that the public is uneasy. If the Bush administration objects to being compared with the Nazi elite, perhaps it should act less like it.

Too much sad history has been told over the centuries by those who failed to speak plainly and forcefully when the times demanded it.

What the Republicans are doing to America and the world has been seen before. And it's been stopped before, but only by facing reality.

Speaking Truth to illegitimate power makes dictatorships temporary. That's the only way the SuperPower of Peace can ultimately prevail... which it will.

ABOUT THE AUTHORS

Harvey Wasserman is a senior advisor to Greenpeace USA and the Nuclear Information & Resource Service, author or co-author of six books, including four on nuclear power and renewable energy, and two histories of the United States, and senior editor of www.freepress.org and the journal the *Columbus Free Press*.

Wasserman's writings and columns have appeared in major newspapers and magazines worldwide. He has worked as a radio talk show host and has appeared on hundreds of radio and TV programs over the years. He has also spoken to several hundred campus and citizen gatherings for peace, justice and environmental sanity, and is a member of the National Writers Union, Local 1981 of the United Auto Workers.

After graduating from the University of Michigan in 1967, Wasserman helped found the legendary anti-war Liberation News Service, which in 1968 moved to the Montague (Massachusetts) Farm, still in operation as one of the longest-standing organic communal farms in U.S. history.

In 1973 Montague became a launching pad for the grassroots anti-nuclear movement. Wasserman helped coin the phrase "No Nukes" in the successful fight against twin reactors proposed nearby. In 1976 he helped organize the Clamshell Alliance, which staged the first mass demonstrations against the Seabrook nuclear plant. In 1979 he co-organized the Musicians United for Safe Energy (MUSE) concerts in Madison Square Garden. In 1994 he spoke for Greenpeace to 350,000 semi-conscious fans at Woodstock 2.

Along the way Wasserman has taught history and journalism at

Hampshire College, earned an M.A. in U.S. history from the University of Chicago, and traveled around the world, speaking and writing against nuclear power. He moved to central Ohio in the mid 1980s, where he has helped organize successful campaigns against a regional radioactive waste dump, a trash-burning power plant, a cancelled housing development near a wetlands wildlife refuge, and the now-defunct (and internationally infamous) McDonald's restaurant in his home community of Bexley.

Most recently Wasserman has focused on the rising renewable energy industry. In 2002 he co-authored, with legendary wind power pioneer Dan Juhl, *Harvesting Wind Energy as a Cash Crop: A Guide to Locally Owned Wind Farming*. He hopes to convert Ohio and the world to a "solartopia" of wind and solar power.

Bob Fitrakis is a Political Science Professor at Columbus State Community College, where he won the Distinguished Teaching Award in 1991. He was a Ford Foundation Fellow to the Michigan State legislature in 1975 and studied at the University of Sarajevo on scholarship in 1978. Fitrakis earned a J.D. from the Ohio State University College of Law and his Ph.D. in Political Science from Wayne State University in Detroit.

Fitrakis was a member of the Human Rights Party in Michigan, a founding member of the Michigan Democratic Socialists Caucus, a founding member of the Democratic Socialists of America and the Democratic Socialists of Central Ohio. He served on the National Political Committee of DSA in 1994 and 1995.

Fitrakis was a candidate for Congress in 1992, running against Congressman John Kasich, and he was an elected Democratic Party ward committeeperson from 1996 to 2000.

In March 1994 he served as an international observer for the national elections in El Salvador and in 1993 he visited Reynosa and Matamoros, Mexico, as part of a human rights delegation to investigate conditions in the maquilladoras. As a result of the trip, he co-produced a video titled "The Other Side of Free Trade" shown around the country at colleges and on public access TV stations. In 2003, the Native American Indian Center of Central Ohio honored him with their Selma Walker Award for Lifetime Achievement in Human Rights Activism.

Fitrakis is the Executive Director of the Columbus Institute for Contemporary Journalism and has published the *Free Press* since 1992 and acted as editor since 1993. From 1996 to 2002, Fitrakis was a columnist and investigative reporter for *Columbus Alive*, a local alternative weekly newspaper, and earned numerous journalism awards from the Society of Professional Journalists, Press Club of Cleveland and Association of Alternative Newsweeklies. He has also written for other national and local publications, has co-hosted a news and public affairs program on public access television, and currently hosts a call-in talk radio show.

He is the author of *The Fitrakis Files* series of books, compilations of his writings at the *Free Press* and *Columbus Alive*. Fitrakis also wrote *The Idea of Democratic Socialism in America and the Decline of the Socialist Party* (Garland Publishers, 1993). He is a frequent speaker on political, labor and social policy issues at national academic and political conferences.

Printed in the United States
23091LVS00006B/209

9 780971 043848